SUBSIDIZING SHELTER

The Relationship between Welfare and Housing Assistance

URBAN INSTITUTE REPORT 1

Sandra J. Newman
Ann B. Schnare

█▌ THE URBAN INSTITUTE PRESS
Washington, D.C.
May 1988

Sandra J. Newman is the Associate Director for Research, Institute for Policy Studies, Johns Hopkins University, an Associate Professor in the Department of Geography and Environmental Engineering, and a Visiting Fellow at The Urban Institute. In addition to the analysis of housing needs and housing policy, her research focuses on long-term care. She holds a Ph.D. in Urban Planning from New York University.

Ann B. Schnare, Vice-President for Housing and Real Estate at ICF, Inc. is an economist specializing in housing market analysis and policy research. She was director of The Urban Institute Center for Public Finance and Housing between 1983 and 1987 and holds a Ph.D. in economics from Harvard University.

THE URBAN INSTITUTE PRESS
2100 M Street, N.W.
Washington, D.C. 20037

Kathleen A. Lynch
    Director
Christopher N. Clary
    Publishing Assistant

Printed in the
United States of America.

9 8 7 6 5 4 3 2 1

Distributed by
University Press of America
4720 Boston Way
Lanham, MD 20706

Library of Congress Cataloging in
Publication Data
p. c.m.(Urban Institute Reports)
Contents: Part 1 Analysis and
findings--Part 2 Data book
ISSN 0897-7399
ISBN 0-87766-414-5
1. Poor--Housing--United States
2. Public welfare--United States
3. Housing policy--United States
I. Schnare, Ann Burnet
II. Title. III. Series.
HD7287.96.U6N48 1987
363.5'8--dc19
87-34026 CIP

URBAN INSTITUTE REPORTs are used to disseminate significant research findings and analysis arising out of the work of The Urban Institute. To reduce costs and minimize production delays, these reports are produced with desktop publishing technology. Like all publications of The Urban Institute Press, each Urban Institute Report is reviewed rigorously in an effort to uphold the highest standards of policy research and analysis.

The Urban Institute is a nonprofit policy research and educational organization established in Washington, D.C., in 1968. Its staff investigates the social and economic problems confronting the nation and government policies and programs designed to alleviate such problems. The Institute disseminates significant findings of its research through the publications program of its Press. The Institute has two goals for work in each of its research areas: to help shape thinking about societal problems and efforts to solve them, and to improve government decisions and performance by providing better information and analytic tools.

Through work that ranges from broad conceptual studies to administrative and technical assistance, Institute researchers contribute to the stock of knowledge available to public officials and private individuals and groups concerned with formulating and implementing more efficient and effective government policy.

Conclusions or opinions expressed in Institute publications are those of the authors and do not necessarily reflect the views of other staff members, officers or trustees of the Institute, advisory groups, or any organizations that provide financial support to the Institute.

ACKNOWLEDGEMENTS

We gratefully acknowledge the capable research assistance of Michael Heller, Spencer Johnson, Marc Solomon and Mittie Olion, and the computer assistance of Kirk O'Neal, Isolde Spiegel, Paul Wright, Mark Friedman, Timothy Dilauro, Miguel Cordova, and Peter Kroll. We would also like to thank the numerous state and local welfare administrators who provided much of the basic data presented in this report. We have benefited from the comments of Greg Duncan, Marilyn Moon and other colleagues who participated in the 1985 Association of Public Policy and Management (APPAM) Seminar on "New Evidence on Welfare Policy and Behavior," from Amy Jones', Sara Johnson's, and David Bryson's insights on HUD treatment of welfare shelter subsidies, from Jack Kerry's admonitions on housing programs, from the ever-stimulating and encouraging dialogue with Mary Nenno, and from the comments of two anonymous reviewers. Finally, we would like to thank Felicity Skidmore for editing the report, and Marie Kuhn, Marsha Somers, and Christopher Clary for their tireless efforts in producing it.

CONTENTS

viii

ABSTRACT

This study examines the relationship between income and housing assistance programs. The welfare system, through the explicit and implicit shelter allowances that welfare recipients receive as part of their public assistance benefits, spends at least $10 billion a year on housing assistance--roughly the same as the Department of Housing and Urban Development. Yet the two streams of government financing for low income housing are uncoordinated and frequently overlapping.

Part 1 presents new evidence on both the nature and the impact of this two-pronged approach to providing shelter assistance to the poor. It compares the level of benefits available to households receiving various combinations of aid, and documents the housing outcomes that are produced by the two systems of shelter support.

Part 2 presents detailed statistics on estimated shelter allowances under Aid to Families with Dependent Children (AFDC), Supplemental Security Income (SSI), and General Assistance (GA) for each of the fifty states and the District of Columbia. Subsequent reports will focus on alternative policy strategies for addressing weaknesses in the current system.

PART 1 ANALYSIS AND FINDINGS

EXECUTIVE SUMMARY

As welfare reform moves to a higher priority on the nation's legislative agenda, housing is conspicuous by its absence. The ability to obtain adequate shelter is a basic necessity of life--like food, clothing, and medical care. A welfare system that does not enable recipients to obtain adequate shelter is a failure by any standard. Yet the rising number of homeless families across the country and the incidence of welfare recipients living in substandard units suggest such a failure. This report documents the problems of the current housing system as identified by the first phase of The Urban Institute's Welfare and Housing Project. The second phase will develop strategies for reform.

THE HOUSING GAP

There is a large and growing gap between the demand and supply of affordable units. In 1983, for example, about 9.7 million renters had incomes below $8,000 a year. Using standard definitions of affordability, such households could afford to pay no more than $200 each month on housing. But only 5.3 million units had rents below this level, and 20 percent of these were in substandard condition. Since at least some of the sound, inexpensive units are occupied by richer households, a conservative estimate of the additional units needed if the poor are to be adequately housed is 5.5 million.

Given the current status of federal housing policy, it is unlikely that these housing needs can be met. Cutbacks initiated under the Reagan administration have virtually eliminated all production programs. The Department of Housing and Urban Development (HUD) has reduced its new commitments for assisted housing from over $30 billion to $10 billion a year. Existing contracts for assisted units, which typically last for 15 years, will begin to expire in the early 1990s, making current expenditure levels even more susceptible to future cuts. The tax advantages associated with the development and rehabilitation of low-income housing under the 1986 tax reform could add another $2.7 billion of housing subsidies over the next five years, but this is subject to substantial uncertainty. Where will the necessary resources be found to provide minimally decent housing for the nation's poor who are now without it? Both sides of the political spectrum appear stymied by the high costs of traditional approaches, coupled with the spending constraints imposed by the federal budget deficit.

TWO-PRONGED APPROACH TO HOUSING ASSISTANCE

Policy debates on housing almost uniformly ignore a second source of housing assistance. The welfare system--through the explicit and implicit shelter allowances provided under Aid to Families with Dependent Children (AFDC), Supplemental Security Income (SSI), and General Assistance (GA)--spends at least $10 billion a year on housing assistance, about as much as HUD.

In reality, then, there are two streams of government financing of low-income housing: a housing stream and a welfare stream. The problem is that this approach to shelter assistance through a mix of income maintenance and housing programs is largely uncoordinated, raising serious questions regarding the efficiency, equity, and overall effectiveness of the system.

Efficiency. The involvement of two federal agencies and many states and localities in the provision of shelter assistance raises the probability of inefficiencies, which could arise in three ways: if the goals of the two systems are inconsistent, if the goals overlap, or if the clienteles overlap. Recent shifts in HUD assistance policies suggest that the second and third characterizations are both valid.

Federal involvement in low-income housing began in the depression years, with the creation of the Public Housing Program. Up until the mid-1970s, the primary goal of this and other assistance programs was to increase the supply of standard housing through a variety of approaches involving slum clearance, new construction, and rehabilitation. Following the Nixon Administration's moratorium on housing programs in 1973, however, a very different strategy was introduced: housing certificates to qualified households renting units from the existing stock.   By the early 1980s, essentially all new construction and rehabilitation programs were terminated, leaving the cash certificate for existing housing as HUD's main assistance approach.

Public assistance programs administered by HHS in combination with the states also provide cash grants to eligible households.   The standard of need on which the grant is based represents each state's estimate of the cost of basic necessities, including shelter.   Regardless of the exact amount that recipients spend on housing, the parallel to the current HUD approach seems clear: cash assistance to low-income households to cover shelter costs of housing from the standing stock.

There is also considerable overlap in the clienteles of the two types of programs.   In 1983, for example, nearly one-quarter of the welfare population also received a housing subsidy.   Some 4.6 million households were receiving income assistance alone; 2.1 million were receiving housing subsidies, but not income assistance; and 1.3 million were receiving both.   By 1986, the number in assisted housing had grown to over 4 million households.   Since housing programs are increasingly being targeted to very low-income households, the overlap between HUD and HHS clientele is undoubtedly increasing.

Equity.   The current system of shelter assistance is also unfair. The major welfare programs essentially guarantee that program recipients will live in substandard housing and that similar individuals in different locations will not be treated equally.   Nationally, shelter allowances under welfare cover only a fraction of the cost of modest housing (as measured by HUD Fair Market Rents, or FMR).   AFDC recipients receive shelter allowances that average only about 50 percent of the FMR.   SSI and GA recipients receive allowances that cover 64 and 68 percent, respectively, of the cost of standard housing.

Shelter payment generosity also varies dramatically by location, with the lowest payment levels consistently in the South.   Under AFDC, shelter allowances average only about 27 percent of the FMR in the South, compared to a high of 64 percent in the West.   Under GA, shelter allowances range from 35 percent in the South to 77 percent in the Northeast.   Even under SSI, with the least regional variation, shelter allowances average about 62 percent of the cost of standard housing in the South, compared to about 71 percent in the Northeastern states.

HUD programs, in contrast, are designed to insure that recipients obtain standard housing regardless of location and provide subsidies up to the full amount of the FMR. Unlike the welfare programs, however, households are assisted on a "first come-first served" basis, and only a fraction of the eligible population can be served. There are 2.8 million renters on welfare who do not receive housing assistance but who have incomes that are just as low as those receiving multiple subsidies.

Effectiveness. Finally, the existing system of shelter support is ineffective. Housing assistance recipients generally have decent and affordable dwellings. In contrast, 46 percent of all welfare households spend more than half their income on housing, 13 percent are overcrowded, and 29 percent live in physically substandard units. Eight out of every 10 households with income assistance but no housing program subsidies have at least one of these housing problems. Furthermore, welfare recipients in metropolitan areas with generous shelter allowances often fare no better than the average. As a result, many communities are spending relatively large sums of money with little tangible return on their higher investments.

RESTRUCTURING THE CURRENT SYSTEM

What should a restructured shelter assistance policy look like? While development of detailed policy strategies must await the second phase of the project, some general directions are clear.

First, the new structure must be more equitable than the one it replaces. Neither the welfare system nor the housing system ranks high on equity grounds. Under welfare, there is enormous variation in the housing subsidies received by households both within and between programs. Under housing programs, as a general rule, households are assisted on a first come-first served basis. In 1983 there were eight million renters on welfare who did not receive housing program assistance but who had incomes that were just as low as those participating in housing programs. There are also inequities associated with multiple subsidies: roughly 1.3 million households received both welfare and housing subsidies.

One way the inequities in the current system could be addressed is by reducing or eliminating the regional disparities in welfare payments. This general theme has been echoed in recent proposals addressing the disparities in AFDC benefits.

The appropriate benefit level for such a standardized welfare system is obviously subject to debate. If HUD's shelter standards are used as a criterion, shelter allowances under the major welfare programs would have to be raised by between 50 and 100 percent, depending on the state, to meet them. Our data suggest that this increase would cost about $10 billion a year. If HUD continued to serve a significant number of recipients who were not on welfare, this modification would appear to require an increase in total expenditures on housing assistance (including indirect subsidies available through welfare) of roughly 50 percent.

A more equitable distribution of benefits can be achieved in various ways. One option would be to develop a two-tiered payment system. The full shelter allowance would be available to households in units meeting program standards. A lower subsidy would be paid to households who cannot find, or do not choose, a standard unit, with the understanding that if program standards are met, the full subsidy would be paid. If the lower payment standard were about the same as the current national average (about 60 percent of the FMR), the program's costs would probably drop to about $7 billion per year.

But reducing the regional disparities in welfare payments is not sufficient to insure the equity of shelter assistance policy. Two inequities would still remain: double subsidies for some, and HUD subsidies for only a subset of the eligible population. Resolving these problems will undoubtedly require much closer coordination between housing and welfare policy, funding and personnel than has existed in the past. Such coordination could improve the efficiency and effectiveness of shelter assistance policy, as well as its equity.

The foregoing discussion assumes that housing goals remain a part of the nation's public policy agenda. Judging by the events of the last several years, this is not at all clear. There has not been a federal housing act for several years, virtually all HUD construction subsidy programs have been terminated, funding for existing demand-side programs is meager, and the 1986 tax reform legislation makes the future of private sector involvement in the provision of low-income housing uncertain at best.

We believe a case can be made for restructuring housing policy. This case rests on several factors: the inequities and inefficiencies of the current two-pronged system, the ineffectiveness of welfare programs at achieving housing goals, the realization that transfer payments earmarked for housing are substantially different form untied income transfers, and most fundamentally, the motivations that underlie society's support for programs that assist the poor. We believe the case is compelling.

1

INTRODUCTION

For most families and particularly the poor, housing is the single biggest item in the monthly budget. It may also represent the highest priority item since failure to pay each month's rent will result ultimately in eviction.

The housing problems of the poor are deep and tangled (1; 2). In 1983, for example, about 9.7 million renters had incomes below $8,000 a year. Using standard definitions of affordability, such households could afford to pay no more than $200 a month for housing. But in that same year, only 5.3 million occupied units had rents below this level, and 20 percent of these were in substandard condition. This large and growing gap between the demand and supply of affordable units lies at the heart of the housing problems of the poor.

Despite the apparent need, the country's low-income housing policy is in disarray. Cutbacks initiated under the Reagan administration have virtually eliminated all production programs, and HUD's new commitments for assisted housing have dropped from over $30 to $10 billion a year. Existing contracts for assisted units, which typically last for 15 years, will begin to expire in the early 1990s, making current expenditure levels more susceptible to future cuts. And there is substantial uncertainty regarding the future development of low-income units under the 1986 tax reform.

While the current system is undoubtedly ripe for reform, there is no consensus on the changes that need to be made. Liberals, moderates, and conservatives alike appear to be stymied by the high costs of traditional approaches, coupled with the lack of federal resources. There is growing recognition that the existing approach to meeting the housing needs of the poor is fragmented at best, and

7

inequitable and inefficient at worst. Yet relatively little is known about ways in which traditional housing assistance programs interact with other aspects of the welfare system or, more fundamentally, about how best to spend scarce public resources on providing decent housing for the poor.

THE TWO-PRONGED APPROACH TO HOUSING ASSISTANCE

The current approach to housing assistance is an interrelated but largely uncoordinated mix of direct and indirect subsidies available to households and owners of housing projects. On the housing side there are two major programs. The U.S. Department of Housing and Urban Development (HUD) now spends about $10 billion a year on assisted housing.[1] In addition, tax advantages associated with the development and rehabilitation of low-income housing under the 1986 tax reforms could result in another $2.7 billion of subsidies over the next five years (3). This is not, however, the only type of housing assistance. The welfare system is the second source, which typically has been overlooked in the formulation of housing policy. Our estimates suggest that the welfare system--through the explicit and implicit shelter allowances provided under Aid to Families with Dependent Children (AFDC), Supplemental Security Income (SSI), and General Assistance (GA)--spends at least $10 billion a year on housing assistance, about as much as HUD.[2]

Thus, in reality there are two streams of government financing of low-income housing: a housing stream and a welfare stream. Government involvement in this activity is shared by two federal agencies, HUD and the U.S. Department of Health and Human Services (HHS), plus a multiplicity of states and local jurisdictions. But their approaches are uncoordinated and potentially overlapping. This two-pronged approach to shelter assistance raises serious questions regarding the equity, efficiency and overall effectiveness of the existing system.

Equity. Under traditional income maintenance programs, geography rather than need plays the major role in determining the amount of shelter assistance that an individual or family receives, and even in the most generous parts of the country, the amount provided falls far short of the amount required. Recent rough estimates of the relationship between AFDC shelter allowances in different states and the costs of modest housing (4) indicate the shelter allowances covered between 12 and 77 percent of the amount required to obtain a standard unit in the rental market (as measured by HUD's estimated fair market rent or FMR).[3] All but seven states allocated less than 50 percent. Families lucky enough to be enrolled in an assisted housing program, in contrast, receive a subsidy equal to the full amount of their shelter needs.

Efficiency. The involvement of two separate federal agencies and many states and localities in the provision of shelter assistance raises the probability of inefficiencies, which could arise in three ways: if the goals of the two systems are inconsistent, if the goals overlap, or if the clienteles overlap. Recent shifts in HUD assistance policies suggest that the second and third characterizations are both valid.

Federal involvement in the housing sector began in the depression years, with the establishment of the Federal Housing Agency (FHA) and the creation of the Public Housing Program. Up until the mid-1970s, the main goals of Public Housing and other assistance programs were to increase the supply of standard housing and improve housing conditions for the poor. Implementing these goals involved slum clearance, new construction, and rehabilitation programs. After the 1973 housing assistance moratorium of the Nixon administration, however, a very different implementation strategy was introduced: housing certificates to qualified households who rent housing units from the existing stock.[4] By the early 1980s, essentially all new construction and rehabilitation programs were terminated, leaving the cash certificate for existing housing as HUD's main assistance approach. Since this assistance is targeted to families with very low incomes, it is almost certain to overlap with the welfare clientele of HHS.

Public assistance programs administered by HHS in combination with the states, such as AFDC, provide cash grants to eligible households. The standard of need on which the grant is based represents each state's estimate of the cost of basic necessities such as food, clothing, and shelter. Thus, regardless of the amount recipients actually spend on shelter, the parallel to HUD's current approach to housing assistance seems clear: welfare provides cash assistance to low-income households to cover shelter costs of housing from the standing stock. While a few communities have attempted to leverage the sizable pool of dollars available through the welfare system to rehabilitate their housing stock, for the most part the potential linkage between housing assistance and income support has not been exploited.

Effectiveness. While HUD programs impose minimum quality standards on the housing of its recipients, HHS programs do not. As a result, there is serious concern that the welfare population resides in deplorable housing, possibly even in communities where shelter allowances are relatively high. At a minimum, this suggests that a substantial pool of taxpayer dollars is supporting inadequate housing. Indeed, our analysis suggests that the housing conditions of welfare recipients often bear little relationship to the generosity of the shelter allowances they receive. As a result, many communities are expending relatively large sums of money with little return on their higher investments.

Arguments about effectiveness are also beginning to emerge in recent discussions about the growing incidence of the homeless. Alcoholism, combined with the deinstitutionalization of the chronically mentally ill, undoubtedly accounts for much of the homelessness that exists today. Nevertheless, there is anecdotal evidence that Emergency Assistance, which is designed to provide temporary shelter to individuals with no other place to go, is increasingly used by families with chronic housing needs. Such assistance is extremely expensive and does little to improve the long-term housing situation of the nation's poor.

STUDY OBJECTIVES

All estimates point to dramatically rising rents in the next few years, further exacerbating the problem of an inadequate supply of affordable units for the poor and the middle class. The growing inability of families to pay for shelter, combined with a substantial loss of low cost units from the housing stock, argue for a rethinking of government's role in housing assistance. This report takes a step in that direction.

It is important to recognize at the outset that we focus on the assisted population: that is, households receiving either income or housing assistance. This group does not define the universe of individuals with a housing need. For example, we do not examine the homeless population which, by conservative estimates, numbers about 300,000 nationwide. Nor have we focused on households with incomes below the poverty line who are not receiving government aid. In 1983, the number of such households (8.5 million) was higher than the number of households receiving either income support or housing assistance (8.0 million).

The welfare population (defined as those with income assistance, but no housing subsidy) does not have a monopoly on housing problems (table 1.1). A relatively high proportion of unassisted households with incomes below the poverty line live in physically deficient or crowded units. While they are better off than the welfare population on both of these measures, they are worse off in terms of affordability. Some 78 percent of the unassisted poor pay more than 30 percent of their incomes for housing, and 60 percent pay more than half. This pattern could well reflect the more temporary nature of their impoverishment, but their current needs are nevertheless very real in both absolute and relative terms.

By focusing solely on assisted households, our analysis can only provide information on how well the current shelter assistance system functions for those who actually receive its services. The broader issue of whom should be served by government programs is left for another forum.

CONTENTS OF REPORT

The remainder of this report is organized into three chapters. Chapter 2 presents a detailed description of the treatment of shelter assistance under the three principal welfare programs: AFDC, SSI, and GA. The data were obtained from telephone surveys of state and local welfare administrators and reviews of program documents. In addition to presenting information on the implicit and explicit shelter allowances provided by the different programs, we compare these shelter allowances to the cost of "decent but modest" housing as determined by HUD.

Chapter 3 takes a broad look at the overlap between housing assistance and traditional welfare programs using a national data base, the 1983 American Housing Survey (AHS). We examine the number and types of households currently receiving income assistance and direct rental subsidies, the overlap between the two groups, and the housing conditions of each. We also take a detailed look at the welfare population in 25 specific metropolitan areas surveyed in separate Standard Metropolitan Statistical Area (SMSA) studies by the AHS, in order to relate their housing conditions to the generosity of their shelter allowances.

The final chapter draws some general conclusions about the strengths and weaknesses of the current system. Based on the evidence

Table 1.1   HOUSING CONDITIONS BY POVERTY STATUS AND TYPE OF
ASSISTANCE, 1983 (percent unless otherwise indicated)

| Category | Assisted households | | Unassisted households | |
	Housing assistance[a]	Income assistance only[b]	Poor	Non-poor
Number of households (thousands)	3,392	4,568	8,540	68,244
Unaffordable housing[c]	39.6	66.8	77.7	23.9
Substandard units	8.0	28.5	19.4	6.3
Crowded units[d]	6.2	13.3	8.4	2.0
At least one housing problem	47.2	78.2	86.1	30.9

a. Includes households receiving both income and housing assistance.
b. Excludes households with both income and housing assistance.
c. Unaffordable units are defined as units having costs (excluding utilities) that exceed 30 percent of household income.
d. Crowded units are defined as units with more than one person per room.

of our own analysis and that of the housing policy literature, we raise the policy questions that will need to be answered before the nation's approach to housing assistance can be restructured.

Notes

1.   This estimate excludes expenditures under the Community Development Block Grant program, the Housing Development Action Grant (HODAG) program, public housing modernization, and the like.

2.   We estimate that in fiscal 1984, AFDC allocated roughly $5.2 billion to shelter assistance, SSI allocated roughly $3.4 billion, and General Assistance roughly $1.4 billion. The first and third estimates are based on state data we collected; the second is derived by multiplying total fiscal 1984 SSI payments by the fraction of those payments estimated to be devoted to shelter costs (see table 2.2 in chapter 2).

3.   HUD establishes a Fair Market Rent (or FMR) for Standard Metropolitan Statistical Areas and non-urban counties in the U.S. The FMR represents HUD's estimate of the cost of a standard rental unit in each jurisdiction.

4.   These certificates are currently valued at the difference between the rental cost of a standard apartment and 30 percent of the household's income.

2

SHELTER ALLOWANCES UNDER THE WELFARE SYSTEM

In this chapter, we take a close look at the shelter allowances embedded in general welfare programs. Since we estimate that these subsidies account for slightly more than half of all monies flowing into shelter assistance, and affect more than twice as many recipients as are affected by traditional housing assistance programs, this examination of welfare shelter subsidies is long overdue.

STATE TREATMENT OF SHELTER ASSISTANCE UNDER AFDC

AFDC is the means-tested program for single parents with dependent children. As noted below, a minority of states extend AFDC under the Unemployed Parent (UP) segment to include eligible two-parent families. Nine states set explicit dollar maximums as their estimates of what shelter actually costs in their jurisdiction ("shelter need") and explicit dollar maximums for the shelter grant the recipient will actually receive ("shelter payment").[1] Shelter costs that fall below this ceiling are fully subsidized. If the AFDC household's actual rent (plus utilities) is greater than this explicit maximum, it must pay for this additional shelter cost out of pocket.

The rest of the states do not make explicit shelter grants. Instead, they use consolidated need standards and payment levels. While these consolidated standards may have originally been based on estimates of the actual cost of food, clothing and shelter, these underlying estimates never come into play. Recipients receive a consolidated payment as their welfare grant with no particular fraction earmarked for any particular component of need.

For purposes of analysis, we have divided states into three groupings based on our ability to estimate the shelter portion of the

13

welfare grant from available state data. The first group includes the nine states that use explicit shelter maximums plus another fifteen states for which we are able to estimate with reasonable precision the portion of the AFDC grant devoted to shelter.

The second group consists of another nine states for which we can derive an implicit shelter standard from several pieces of information although there is no single, explicitly stated amount. In some instances, a different overall standard of need (and payment level) is established for individuals who have no housing costs (e.g., individuals who live rent-free with another family); shelter needs and payment levels can be derived by comparing the grants available to such families to the grants available to families that must pay for housing. In others, states were able to give us a rough percentage of the standard of need and payment level that was devoted to shelter.

The third group consists of the remaining states, which provide only aggregate amounts for needs standards and payment levels; there is no way to derive, either explicitly or implicitly, the amount allocated to shelter. In order to include these states in the national analysis, we set their ratio of shelter need to standard of need (and shelter payment to payment level ratio) at 30 percent, which represents a rough average of these ratios for the thirty-three states with either explicit or derived shelter assistance components.[2]

Before turning to a detailed discussion of the differences between the states in their approach to shelter assistance under AFDC, we should note several more general differences that are at least equally important. First, only twenty-one states (roughly 41 percent) provide assistance payments to eligible households at 100 percent of the state's own established needs standard (i.e., the cost of basic necessities the state deems are required to maintain a minimum standard of living). The rest pay some arbitrary fraction which falls as low as 31 percent. The same is true of the relationship between the standard set for shelter by the state and the actual shelter payment that is made to eligible households.

These state variations result in striking regional contrasts, as shown in table 2.1. The South ranks lowest on all four indicators shown. For example, the South's standard of need is 20 percent lower than that of the Northeast, which has the next lowest need standard. The comparison of shelter payment levels is even more dramatic; here, the South's payment is, on average, only about half as much as that in the North Central region and about one-third that in the West. The West is almost consistently at the high end of the range.

Table 2.1   AFDC CHARACTERISTICS, BY REGION, 1984-85 (dollars)

	Standard of need	Shelter need	Payment level	Shelter payment
Northeast	450	177	391	159
North Central	528	178	361	121
South	363	115	201	64
West	535	210	487	189

Note: The national family size distribution was applied to each state to derive regional averages for these indicators (see volume II, appendix A for derivation). Maximum AFDC payments are used in all calculations. These estimates are calculated from information obtained in telephone interviews with state AFDC officials and state documents.

Another source of contrast is the large difference in the depth of subsidy to households under AFDC versus HUD housing assistance. In fifteen jurisdictions around the country, the total AFDC payment received by a family of four, which is supposed to cover the cost of *all* basic necessities including shelter, is smaller than the *lowest* Fair Market Rent (FMR) within the state. In another twenty-two jurisdictions, the AFDC payment is less than one-and-a-half times the lowest FMR.[3]

Beyond these broad patterns, states differ in at least six additional ways in how they determine the level of shelter assistance a household will receive: (a) adjustments for family size; (b) adjustments for location within a state (e.g., higher versus lower cost areas); (c) fraction of the needs standard devoted to shelter; (d) fraction of shelter needs actually covered (i.e., the ratio of shelter payment to shelter need); (e) relationship between shelter payments and the actual costs of standard housing (as measured by the HUD FMRs); and (f) frequency of updates to shelter payment levels. Highlights of each of these disparities are described below. Full detail is shown in Appendix A.

Adjustments for Family Size. Ten states make no distinction in the shelter payments provided to families of three versus four persons.[4] In one state (Illinois) the shelter payment actually is reduced for larger family sizes. In the remaining states, the difference in shelter payments by family size ranges from a low of one percent (Florida) to a high of 29 percent (Oklahoma). Since larger families require larger, more expensive dwelling units, they are disadvantaged relative to smaller families in states where the payment differential is relatively low.

Differentials by Intra-State Location. Ten states differentiate their shelter payment levels geographically, recognizing the variation in housing costs by market area. The remaining forty-one apply a single shelter payment level to all locations. Since housing costs are typically higher in urban areas, this creates significant disparities in the effective value of the shelter supplement in urban versus rural areas.

Shelter Need: Standard of Need. There is also a marked variation in the proportion of the needs standard which states allocate to shelter, and this differentiation varies further by family size. For one-person families, the states' estimate of shelter needs ranges from about 20 percent of the total needs standard in Iowa to about 52 percent of total needs in New York City and the state of Washington. At the other extreme of family size (not shown here), Arkansas devotes the smallest proportion of its needs standard to shelter for six-person families (about 12 percent), while Washington again assigns the highest fraction (about 49 percent). Furthermore, states vary in the extent to which they differentiate these ratios by family size; South Dakota, for example, has nearly a 40 percentage point differential between one-person and six-person families; some states differentiate little, if at all.

Fraction of Shelter Need Actually Covered. The percentage of shelter need that is translated into a shelter payment for AFDC recipients also varies widely across the states (see also appendix A). Twenty-two states (about 43 percent of all states) fund their total shelter need standard, while most of the remaining states fund at least 50 percent of the shelter standard. Six states, however, fund less than half of the standard.

Deviation of Shelter Payment from FMR. Comparing shelter payments for four-person AFDC families to the lowest FMR in a state understates the discrepancy between AFDC shelter payments and HUD FMRs. Even this comparison reveals substantial differences, however; it also demonstrates the shallowness of the AFDC shelter subsidy. Seven states[5] use shelter payments that are 20 percent or less of the lowest FMR for any location within their jurisdiction. AFDC shelter payments in another twenty-seven states fall somewhere between 21 and 50 percent of the lowest FMR. Only the state of Washington funds shelter payments that are virtually as high as the lowest FMR in the state.

Updating over Time. The striking disparities between shelter payments and FMRs may result in part from the great time lags between updates of the AFDC need standards or payment levels. Few states attempt such updating on a regular basis. In a number of states, the last review of standards occurred at least five years ago. In some instances, even when adjustments are made, they do not necessarily bring the standard up to current prices. For example, Georgia last updated its standard of need in 1980, but values were inflated to equal only 90 percent of *1969* estimates. It is also important to realize that even if adjustments are proposed by state AFDC program staff, it is ultimately the legislature that makes the final budgetary decisions regarding funding levels. In the face of budget pressures, recommendations to update standards and payments on a regular basis may be futile.

Additional Variations. In addition to the six variations already discussed, which directly affect the amount of cash assistance a recipient receives, several other types of disparities between jurisdictions are worth mentioning. First, states vary in the proportion of AFDC benefits that are paid for by the federal government. While the statutory minimum federal share must be 50 percent, in FY 1984 it exceeded 70 percent in eleven states. The federal share is determined by a formula which heavily weights state per capita income; thus, roughly 78 percent of Mississippi's AFDC benefits are covered by the federal government compared to 50 percent in New York or California. Appendix B lists the federal share of AFDC benefit payments for all states.

Second, states have some discretion in determining who is eligible to receive AFDC assistance. All states must provide grants to eligible children. But twenty-nine states do not cover needy two-parent families whose principal earner is unemployed, and thirty states do not provide benefits to individuals (other than the mother) who perform an essential service for recipients. (Appendix C illustrates the variation in state eligibility rules.)

STATE TREATMENT OF SHELTER ASSISTANCE UNDER SUPPLEMENTAL SECURITY INCOME (SSI)

SSI is the means-tested income assistance program for the aged, blind, and disabled. In contrast to AFDC, interstate variation in SSI payments for those living in non-institutional, non-group quarter residences is minor because SSI is a federal program. Although most states supplement the federal SSI benefit standard, these supplements are typically small except in the context of special residential settings such as homes for the aged and domiciliary care facilities. For individuals and couples either living independently or in another person's household--the two living arrangements that are distinguished by the federal SSI law--only twenty-eight states provide any supplement at all, and in thirteen of these cases, the amount of the supplement is less than $50 per month.[6] Thus, in twenty-three states, the SSI benefit is financed entirely by the federal government.

Only three states--Connecticut, Nebraska, and Idaho--set explicit shelter maximums under SSI. In each of these jurisdictions, the state has a standard of need and payment level for basic necessities including shelter. The maximum amount set for shelter is actually paid for by a combination of federal and state SSI dollars.

For the remaining states, no explicit shelter needs and payment standards exist. However, because the SSI law explicitly values the cost of living in another person's household at two-thirds the cost of living independently, one approach for estimating the implicit shelter payment incorporated in the SSI grant is to assume that it equals one-third of the total payment (the basic federal benefit plus any supplement provided by the state) made to qualified persons living independently.[7]

It can be argued, however, that for the twenty-five states that do not have explicit shelter payments but do provide state supplements, this approach introduces more uniformity into the SSI program than is warranted. Using the one-third criterion as an upper bound for shelter-related costs is entirely legitimate for the federal portion of the SSI payment. But it may not accurately reflect a particular state's view of what portion of its supplement underwrites the shelter costs of SSI recipients.

For example, of the ten states that provide supplementary payments greater than $50 per month, four make no distinction in their payments to recipients living independently as opposed to living in another's household.[8] Moreover, while three additional states are consistent with the federal statute in that they reduce their payments to those in joint living arrangements, the reduction is not the two-thirds used by the federal government nor is it the same fraction for individuals and couples. Two other states are even more at variance with the federal approach: they *increase* their supplements to recipients living with others.[9]

For this reason we also pursued a second method to estimating shelter payments under SSI, one that explicitly recognizes the variations in the way SSI supplement states approach the shelter component. This state-specific amount is then added to the federal shelter payment component (i.e., one-third of the total payment for those living independently) to produce a total shelter payment for each state.

The last seven columns of table 2.2 show: (a) the range of values for shelter payments produced by these two alternative methods; (b) HUD's estimate of the minimum FMR for an efficiency unit in the state; and (c) the resulting shelter payment to FMR ratios. Since an efficiency apartment is the type of unit for which an eligible individual living alone would qualify under Section 8 program guidelines, the most valid comparison among these figures is between the implicit SSI shelter payment for an individual and the FMR for an efficiency unit.

Table 2.2 SUMMARY STATISTICS ON SHELTER ASSISTANCE UNDER SSI, BY STATE, 1984-85 DATA

Region and state	Number of persons with SSI	Assistance for persons living independently (dollars)				Assistance for persons living in another's household (dollars)			
		Maximum federal and state SSI benefit level		Amount of state supplement		Maximum federal and state SSI benefit level		Amount of state supplement	
		Individual	Couple	Individual	Couple	Individual	Couple	Individual	Couple
Northeast									
Connecticut	23,943	465.70	574.20	140.70	86.20	357.37	411.54	140.70	86.20
Maine	20,684	335.00	503.00	10.00	15.00	224.67	337.34	8.00	12.00
Massachusetts	108,378	453.82	689.72	128.82	201.72	321.03	541.14	104.36	215.80
New Hampshire	5,308	339.00	489.00	14.00	1.00	243.67	346.34	27.00	21.00
New Jersey	85,078	356.25	513.36	31.25	25.36	260.98	418.43	44.31	93.06
New York	336,463	385.91	564.03	60.91	76.03	224.91	352.37	8.24	27.03
Pennsylvania	154,026	357.40	536.70	32.40	48.70	249.07	374.04	32.40	48.70
Rhode Island	14,482	378.80	589.74	53.80	101.74	279.65	440.57	62.98	115.23
Vermont	8,743	378.00	584.50	53.00	96.50	251.97	370.14	35.30	44.80
Total weighted average	757,105	387.07	569.62	62.07	81.62	253.31	394.53	36.64	69.19

Table 2.2 (continued)

Region and state	Number of persons with SSI	Assistance for persons living independently (dollars)				Assistance for persons living in another's household (dollars)			
		Maximum federal and state SSI benefit level		Amount of state supplement		Maximum federal and state SSI benefit level		Amount of state supplement	
		Individual	Couple	Individual	Couple	Individual	Couple	Individual	Couple
North Central									
Illinois	119,761	360.23	521.70	35.23	33.70	251.90	359.04	35.23	33.70
Indiana	40,532	325.00	488.00	0.00	0.00	216.67	325.34	0.00	0.00
Iowa	25,530	347.00	532.00	22.00	44.00	238.67	369.34	22.00	44.00
Kansas	19,549	325.00	488.00	0.00	0.00	216.67	325.34	0.00	0.00
Michigan	110,542	351.70	528.00	26.70	40.00	235.27	353.17	18.60	27.83
Minnesota	29,852	360.00	554.00	35.00	66.00	276.00	484.00	59.33	158.66
Missouri	77,074	325.00	488.00	0.00	0.00	216.67	325.34	0.00	0.00
Nebraska	13,001	386.00	580.00	68.50	99.50	285.17	424.84	68.50	99.50
North Dakota	5,838	325.00	488.00	0.00	0.00	216.67	325.34	0.00	0.00
Ohio	115,324	325.00	488.00	0.00	0.00	216.67	325.34	0.00	0.00
South Dakota	7,663	340.00	503.00	15.00	15.00	231.67	340.34	15.00	15.00
Wisconsin	62,610	424.70	649.00	99.70	161.00	316.37	486.34	99.70	161.00
Total weighted average	627,276	350.29	524.57	25.55	36.73	241.95	364.34	25.28	39.00

Table 2.2 (continued)

Region and state	Number of persons with SSI	Assistance for persons living independently (dollars)				Assistance for persons living in another's household (dollars)			
		Maximum federal and state SSI benefit level		Amount of state supplement		Maximum federal and state SSI benefit level		Amount of state supplement	
		Individual	Couple	Individual	Couple	Individual	Couple	Individual	Couple
South									
Alabama	127,849	325.00	488.00	0.00	0.00	216.67	325.34	0.00	0.00
Arkansas	71,503	325.00	488.00	0.00	0.00	216.67	325.34	0.00	0.00
Delaware	6,893	325.00	488.00	0.00	0.00	216.67	325.34	0.00	0.00
District of Columbia	14,758	340.00	518.00	15.00	30.00	231.67	355.34	15.00	30.00
Florida	170,904	325.00	488.00	0.00	0.00	216.67	324.34	0.00	0.00
Georgia	147,945	325.00	488.00	0.00	0.00	216.67	324.34	0.00	0.00
Kentucky	91,685	325.00	488.00	0.00	0.00	216.67	325.34	0.00	0.00
Louisiana	123,093	325.00	488.00	0.00	0.00	216.67	325.34	0.00	0.00
Maryland	47,197	325.00	488.00	0.00	0.00	216.67	325.34	0.00	0.00
Mississippi	109,063	325.00	488.00	0.00	0.00	216.67	325.34	0.00	0.00
North Carolina	131,937	325.00	488.00	0.00	0.00	216.67	325.34	0.00	0.00
Oklahoma	59,081	385.00	608.00	60.00	120.00	276.67	445.34	60.00	120.00
South Carolina	81,071	325.00	488.00	0.00	0.00	216.67	325.34	0.00	0.00
Tennessee	124,149	325.00	488.00	0.00	0.00	216.67	325.34	0.00	0.00
Texas	244,278	325.00	488.00	0.00	0.00	216.67	325.34	0.00	0.00
Virginia	79,320	325.00	488.00	0.00	0.00	216.67	325.34	0.00	0.00
West Virginia	39,571	325.00	488.00	0.00	0.00	216.67	325.34	0.00	0.00
Total weighted average	1,670,297	327.25	492.51	2.25	4.51	218.92	329.66	2.25	4.51

Table 2.2 (continued)

Region and state	Number of persons with SSI	Assistance for persons living independently (dollars)				Assistance for persons living in another's household (dollars)			
		Maximum federal and state SSI benefit level		Amount of state supplement		Maximum federal and state SSI benefit level		Amount of state supplement	
		Individual	Couple	Individual	Couple	Individual	Couple	Individual	Couple
West									
Alaska	3,015	586.00	859.00	261.00	371.00	482.00	707.00	265.33	381.66
Arizona	29,236	325.00	488.00	0.00	0.00	216.67	325.34	0.00	0.00
California	653,383	504.00	936.00	179.00	448.00	395.67	773.34	179.00	448.00
Colorado	28,366	383.00	766.00	58.00	278.00	274.67	603.34	58.00	278.00
Hawaii	9,980	329.90	496.80	4.90	8.80	221.57	334.14	4.90	8.80
Idaho	7,542	383.00	514.00	58.50	26.00	294.67	371.34	78.00	46.00
Montana	6,678	325.00	488.00	0.00	0.00	216.67	325.34	0.00	0.00
Nevada	6,899	361.40	562.46	36.40	74.46	240.94	374.97	24.27	49.63
New Mexico	24,600	325.00	488.00	0.00	0.00	216.67	325.34	0.00	0.00
Oregon	23,123	326.70	488.00	1.70	0.00	218.37	325.34	1.70	0.00
Utah	7,835	335.00	508.00	10.00	20.00	226.67	345.34	10.00	20.00
Washington	43,730	363.30	525.40	38.30	37.40	229.35	341.91	12.68	16.57
Wyoming	1,796	345.00	528.00	20.00	40.00	236.67	365.34	20.00	40.00
Total weighted average	846,183	469.12	847.71	144.12	359.71	359.56	683.99	142.89	358.65
National total weighted average	3,900,861	373.36	589.68	48.38	101.71	259.81	424.69	43.14	99.43

Table 2.2 (continued)

| | Shelter payments: Methods I and II | | | | | | |
| | 33 percent (living independently) | | 33 percent (federal, living independently) plus x percent (state supplement) | | HUD Fair Market Rent[a] | Method I Fair Market Rent (percent) | Method II Fair Market Rent (percent) |
Region and state	Individual	Couple	Individual	Couple			
Northeast							
Connecticut	155.23	191.40	200[b]	200[b]	239	64.95	83.68
Maine	111.67	167.67	110	166	248	45.03	44.35
Massachusetts	151.27	229.91	133	234[c]	261	57.96	50.96
New Hampshire	113.00	163.00	117[c]	170[c]	269	42.01	43.49
New Jersey	118.75	171.12	123[c]	194[c]	265	44.81	46.42
New York	128.64	188.01	161	212	191	67.35	84.29
Pennsylvania	119.13	178.90	119	179	155	76.86	76.86
Rhode Island	126.27	196.58	133[d]	201[d]	267	47.29	49.81
Vermont	126.00	194.83	126	215	254	49.61	49.61
Total weighted average	129.02	189.87	144	206	208	63.96	71.30

Table 2.2 (continued)

| | Shelter payments: Methods I and II | | | | | | |
| Region and state | 33 percent (living independently) | | 33 percent (federal, living independently) plus x percent (state supplement) | | HUD Fair Market Rent[a] | Method I Fair Market Rent (percent) | Method II Fair Market Rent (percent) |
	Individual	Couple	Individual	Couple			
North Central							
Illinois	120.08	173.90	120	174	169	71.05	71.01
Indiana	108.33	162.67	108	163	205	52.85	52.85
Iowa	115.67	177.33	115	178	201	57.55	57.21
Kansas	108.33	162.67	108	163	159	68.13	68.13
Michigan	117.23	176.00	116	175	208	56.36	55.77
Minnesota	120.00	184.67	120	185	195	61.54	61.54
Missouri	108.33	162.67	108	163	159	68.13	68.13
Nebraska	128.67	193.33	140[b]	175[b]	188	68.44	74.47
North Dakota	108.33	162.67	108	163	207	52.33	52.33
Ohio	108.33	162.67	108	163	155	69.89	69.89
South Dakota	113.33	167.67	113	168	199	56.95	56.78
Wisconsin	141.57	216.33	141[e]	216[e]	188	75.30	75.00
Total weighted average	116.80	174.86	117	174	180	65.65	65.59

Table 2.2 (continued)

Shelter payments: Methods I and II

Region and state	33 percent (living independently)		33 percent (federal, living independently) plus x percent (state supplement)		HUD Fair Market Rent[a]	Method I Fair Market Rent (percent)	Method II Fair Market Rent (percent)
	Individual	Couple	Individual	Couple			
South							
Alabama	108.33	162.67	108	163	176	61.55	61.55
Arkansas	108.33	162.67	108	163	156	69.44	69.44
Delaware	108.33	162.67	108	163	244	44.40	44.40
District of Columbia	113.33	172.67	113	173	319	35.53	35.42
Florida	108.33	162.67	108	163	198	54.71	54.71
Georgia	108.33	162.67	108	163	184	58.88	58.88
Kentucky	108.33	162.67	108	163	169	64.10	64.10
Louisiana	108.33	162.67	108	163	156	69.44	69.44
Maryland	108.33	162.67	108	163	244	44.40	44.40
Mississippi	108.33	162.67	108	163	193	56.13	56.13
North Carolina	108.33	162.67	108	163	170	63.73	63.73
Oklahoma	128.33	202.67	128	203	167	76.85	76.65
South Carolina	108.33	162.67	108	163	194	55.84	55.84
Tennessee	108.33	162.67	108	163	174	62.26	62.26
Texas	108.33	162.67	108	163	167	64.87	64.87
Virginia	108.33	162.67	108	163	183	59.20	59.20
West Virginia	108.33	162.67	108	163	201	53.90	53.90
Total weighted average	109.08	164.17	109	164	180	61.22	61.21

Table 2.2 (continued)

Region and state	Shelter payments: Methods I and II						
	33 percent (living independently)		33 percent (federal, living independently) plus x percent (state supplement)		HUD Fair Market Rent [a]	Method I Fair Market Rent (percent)	Method II Fair Market Rent (percent)
	Individual	Couple	Individual	Couple			
West							
Alaska	195.33	286.33	196[c]	289[c]	403	48.47	48.64
Arizona	108.33	162.67	108	163	233	46.49	46.35
California	168.00	312.00	167	311	237	70.89	70.46
Colorado	127.67	255.33	127	255	214	59.66	55.14
Hawaii	109.97	165.60	110	166	370	29.72	29.73
Idaho	127.67	171.33	118[b]	118[b]	214	59.66	114.80
Montana	108.33	162.67	108	163	225	48.15	48.15
Nevada	120.47	187.49	120	188	297	40.56	40.40
New Mexico	108.33	162.67	108	163	197	54.99	54.99
Oregon	108.90	162.67	109	163	200	54.45	54.50
Utah	111.67	169.33	111	170	192	58.16	57.81
Washington	121.10	175.13	134	184	236	51.31	56.78
Wyoming	115.00	176.00	115	176	214	53.74	53.74
Total weighted average	156.37	282.57	157	283	236	66.50	66.40
National total weighted average	124.45	196.56	128	200	198	63.61	65.00

Source: State documents, telephone interviews with state officials, and *The SSI Program for the Aged, Blind, and Disabled* (Washington, D.C.: Social Security Administration, 1985)(6).

Note: Methods are described in the text.

a. Zero bedroom minimum.
b. Explicit shelter maximum under SSI (both federal and state).
c. States that increase their supplement payment for joint households to reflect costs of caretaking. Shelter payment calculated at 33 percent of the supplement for joint living arrangement.
d. Rhode Island increases its supplement payments for joint households to reflect increased rental costs and costs of caretaking. State welfare officials estimate the shelter component at 40 percent of the payment.
e. Wisconsin officials estimated shelter component at 45 percent of supplement payment for independent living.

In making this comparison, it should be kept in mind that we have used maximum values for SSI and minimum values for the FMR. As with the AFDC and FMR comparison presented earlier, this approach understates the true extent of the difference between the SSI implicit shelter payment and the cost of decent, modest rental housing.

SSI shelter dollars across the nation average roughly two-thirds of the cost of modest housing for a single individual living in an efficiency apartment.[10] There are, of course, regional disparities. SSI shelter payments represent a somewhat smaller fraction of FMRs in the South (61 percent) compared to the other regions, whereas they may be up to 10 percent higher than average in the Northeast. Overall, however, there is considerable regional uniformity, even after taking special efforts to give fair representation to any state variations in shelter payments that may exist.

STATE TREATMENT OF SHELTER ASSISTANCE UNDER GENERAL ASSISTANCE (GA)

GA is the income assistance program for individuals who are needy but ineligible for other welfare programs--most prominently single unemployables, disabled individuals awaiting SSI determinations, and families that do not qualify for AFDC.

By far the greatest disparities, both geographically and in program characteristics, are found in GA. This is not surprising since, in contrast to both AFDC and SSI, GA is entirely non-federal.

In most states, GA assistance parallels AFDC or SSI: a standard of need establishes minimum income subsistence levels for families of different sizes, actual payments typically fall below these standards, payments are available over time with periodic income recertifications, and a detailed set of rules and regulations guide program operations. In a substantial minority of states, however, GA is considerably less "institutionalized" and stable than this description indicates: for example, in ten states, assistance payments are available only on a temporary basis, and in about thirteen states, the payment standard does not appear to be anchored in a true needs standard.

In fiscal 1984, GA programs existed in thirty-eight states. Twenty-six of these were entirely state funded and most of the rest had at least some state funding. Even so, only twenty had statewide program regulations.[11] In the remaining eighteen, fundamental program regulations--such as recipient eligibility rules, the amount of the GA payment and the length of time a recipient can stay on GA--were determined at the county or local level.

In order to estimate the amount of GA dollars that provide shelter assistance to the poor we made a number of simplifying assumptions.

In the twenty states with statewide GA programs, we were able to develop state-level GA characteristics through interviews with state officials and reviews of state budget and research documents.[12] In most of the remaining states we collected information on the one or two counties that accounted for the largest proportion of GA expenditures in the state and inflated these estimates to form state aggregates. For example, Clark and Washoe Counties account for roughly 90 percent of all GA expenditures in Nevada; Harris County (Houston) represents roughly 75 percent of Texas GA expenditures; Dade County covers about 90 percent of GA expenditures in Florida. In the remaining states where there were no obviously dominating counties we relied on interviews with state officials, county welfare administrators, surveys of the Association of County Welfare Directors, and the like to develop a picture of state GA characteristics. Since the states with the largest GA expenditures also tend to be the ones with the most detailed documentation on their programs, any errors in our estimates are unlikely to affect the overall conclusions.

GA programs are about equally divided between those with consolidated payments and those with explicit GA shelter payments.[13] To establish the GA shelter payment per recipient, we used the explicit amount in states where it existed. In most of the remaining states, we relied on a range of sources: pre-consolidation ratio of shelter payment to total GA payment, information from state or county officials, or special state GA studies. In five states, we could only apply the national average ratio of total to shelter GA payments to estimate the actual shelter dollars received by recipients.[14]

Table 2.3 shows the marked variation in GA shelter payments and in the proportion of total GA payments that these shelter amounts represent.[15] The national average GA shelter payment is $129, with payments across the country ranging from a low of $36 in Arizona to a high of $311 in Maine. Even if these two states were eliminated, GA shelter payments would continue to present a wide range, from less than $100 to over $200.

The dispersion in shelter payments is closely related to the dispersion in total GA payments per recipient in all states except Nevada. In contrast to the generally close relationship between total GA payments and the amount that is directed toward shelter costs, however, GA shelter payments bear little resemblance to the minimum FMR in many states. Only in five states--Maine, New York, Nebraska, North Dakota, and Iowa--are shelter payments for a single individual and the FMR for efficiency units roughly equal. In another six states, these GA payments provide at least three-quarters of the estimated cost of minimally standard housing.[16] But in the majority of states the ratio is much lower, and falls to less than 30 percent in six states.[17]

Table 2.3 SUMMARY STATISTICS ON SHELTER ASSISTANCE UNDER GENERAL
ASSISTANCE, BY STATE, FISCAL 1984
(dollars unless otherwise indicated)

Region and state	Payment per person			HUD Fair Market Rent[a]	General Assistance Fair Market Rent (percent)
	Total General Assistance	General Assistance shelter	Percent		
Northeast					
Connecticut	268	176	66.0	239	74.0
Maine	406	311	77.0	248	125.0
Massachusetts	244	169	69.0	261	65.0
New Jersey	200	120	60.0	265	45.0
New York	287	193	67.0	191	101.0
Pennsylvania	177	54	30.0	155	35.0
Rhode Island	276	166	60.0	267	62.0
Total weighted average	250	149	60.0	194	77.0
North Central					
Illinois	154	114	74.0	169	67.0
Iowa	280	210	75.0	201	104.0
Kansas	216	106	49.0	159	67.0
Michigan	218	153	70.0	208	74.0
Minnesota	236	173	73.0	195	89.0
Missouri	80	64	80.0	159	40.0
Nebraska	240	225	94.0	188	120.0
North Dakota	210	200	95.0	207	97.0
Ohio	128	64	50.0	155	41.0
South Dakota	125	50	40.0	199	25.0
Wisconsin	175	78	45.0	188	41.0
Total weighted average	171	111	65.0	179	62.0
South					
Delaware	116	70	60.0	244	29.0
District of Columbia	210	107	51.0	319	34.0
Florida	180	108	60.0	198	55.0
Georgia	225	145	64.0	184	79.0
Kentucky	140	100	71.0	169	59.0
Louisiana	91	55	60.0	156	35.0
Maryland	126	59	47.0	244	24.0
Texas	109	66	61.0	167	40.0
Virginia	157	83	53.0	183	45.0
Total weighted average	144	77	53.0	222	35.0

Table 2.3 (continued)

Region and state	Payment per person				General Assistance Fair Market Rent (percent)
	Total General Assistance	General Assistance shelter	Percent	HUD Fair Market Rent[a]	
West					
Arizona	130	36	28.0	233	15.0
California	228	143	63.0	237	60.0
Hawaii	297	175	59.0	370	47.0
Montana	212	130	61.0	225	58.0
Nevada	228	57	25.0	297	19.0
New Mexico	145	88	61.0	197	45.0
Oregon	212	147	69.0	200	74.0
Utah	217	123	57.0	192	64.0
Washington	303	189	62.0	236	80.0
Wyoming	145	60	41.0	214	28.0
Total weighted average	236	145	61.0	243	60.0
Northeast	250	149	60.0	194	77.0
North Central	171	111	65.0	179	62.0
South	144	77	53.0	222	35.0
West	236	145	61.0	243	60.0
National total weighted average	209	129	62.0	193	67.0

Note: The assumptions underlying this table and additional data limitations appear in appendix D.

a.   Minimum FMR for zero bedroom unit.

HUD TREATMENT OF SHELTER PAYMENTS
UNDER WELFARE PROGRAMS

Variations in shelter assistance for welfare recipients are not limited to those inherent in welfare programs.   Welfare recipients who also participate in HUD housing assistance programs (e.g., public housing, Section 8) are subject to further differential treatment (beyond that associated with their dual participation status).   The main disparity centers on HUD's distinct rules regarding shelter allowances in jurisdictions with explicit shelter grants (called "as paid" states by HUD) where the actual shelter payment is set at a fixed fraction of actual housing costs, up to a maximum.[18,19]   The fraction, or "ratable reduction," is based on the state's budget appropriation for welfare assistance.

In these cases HUD sets a welfare tenant's rent payment in assisted housing as the highest of three estimates: 30 percent of adjusted income,[20] 10 percent of gross income, or welfare payments specifically designated to meet the family's housing costs. HUD interprets the third of these to mean the ratably reduced shelter need standard, *not* the ratably reduced shelter payment. However, the states assume that the HUD estimate is the actual rental cost, calculate a second ratable reduction, and grant this smaller amount to the welfare tenant.[21] The tenants living in assisted housing must then make up the difference between the two.

Several inequities result. First, welfare tenants in these states are disadvantaged relative to other housing assistance recipients. Because the shelter need standard (even if ratably reduced only once) is virtually certain to produce the largest amount of the three calculations, these tenants are assigned a heavier cost burden than all other tenants in subsidized housing since their rent to income ratios exceed the usual HUD maximums. Second, these tenants are disadvantaged relative to welfare recipients in either consolidated payment states or as paid states with no ratable reductions. In consolidated states, such tenants are treated the same as non-welfare tenants in assisted housing; their rental contribution is set at either 30 percent of adjusted or 10 percent of gross income. In other as paid states, the fully funded welfare rent is simply passed through either to the landlord (in the case of Section 8 housing) or to the Public Housing Authority or PHA (in the case of public housing).[22]

This implementation of the welfare rent statute has been challenged in three court cases.[23] Welfare tenants make three key arguments against the current interpretation: (1) it represents an inaccurate reading of the original statute; a correct reading would have HUD set the tenant's rent contribution at the ratably reduced actual payment rather than the theoretical shelter need standard; (2) it results in tenant rent payments that exceed statutory guidelines and intent since amendments to the 1974 Housing and Community Development Act explicitly refer to shelter payments and not shelter need standards; and (3) it singles out this class of welfare tenants for harsher treatment in calculating the tenant rental contribution than other tenants in assisted housing, whether on welfare or not.

HUD disagrees with this reading of the statute and argues that since its interpretation is accurate, one of the only remedies would be to require these states to fully fund their shelter need standard--a requirement that is inconsistent with the discretion given to the states under the Social Security Act. But even if the state's welfare program were noncompliant with this federal law, the question would then become whether one federal statute (the Social Security Act) has primacy over another federal statute (the Housing and Community Development Act).

HUD also introduces two other arguments: that an alternative implementation of the welfare rent statute would create inequities between the state's welfare recipients who live in assisted housing and those who do not;[24] and that in 1983, Congress rejected an amendment that would have overruled HUD's regulation, thereby providing a recent test of congressional intent.

The courts' rulings to date have been inconclusive. In one case (Smith v. Pierce), the court held that HUD's regulations violated the rent statute and ordered that the tenant rental contribution be set at the actual shelter payment (7). However, this case predates Congress' rejection of the 1983 amendment noted earlier. In another case (White v. Pierce), the district court ruled in favor of HUD; the case is now on appeal. The third case focused only on a procedural issue and not on the merits.

The judicial evaluation of the arguments is outside the scope of this report. From a public policy perspective, however, the current implementation of the welfare rent statute seems patently unfair to the narrow class of welfare tenants in assisted housing in ratably reduced as paid states--relative to both non-welfare households receiving housing assistance and other welfare tenants in assisted housing. The fact that other welfare recipients in ratably reduced as paid states who do not receive housing assistance are normally forced to spend well in excess of their actual shelter grants in order to find any private market unit to rent is not an argument to equally disadvantage their counterparts who receive housing assistance. It is an argument to eliminate the more fundamental inequities in the system. But in the absence of sweeping reform, a feasible intermediate remedy for the two as paid states would be for the PHA and public welfare agency to arrive at a negotiated rent for these welfare tenants. A negotiated rent, the remedy of choice in the White decision, is not prohibited by the Housing and Community Development Act of 1974.

Beyond the restricted set of inequities specific to these two states lie additional inequities. For example, although welfare tenants who receive housing assistance in non-ratably reduced as paid states may be indifferent to the implementation of the welfare rent statute because their shelter grant is simply passed through from the welfare agency to the PHA or landlord, it is nevertheless the case that their tenant rental contribution exceeds that of other housing assistance recipients, whether on welfare in a consolidated payment state or not on welfare at all.[25] The welfare rent provision, therefore, makes more or less sense depending upon which groups are compared. Although the pass-through of the welfare rent can be justified on the grounds that this is the shelter allowance available to non-housing assistance recipients, it creates clear inequities between subgroups of housing assistance recipients by setting the housing cost burden of welfare tenants higher than that assigned to other housing assistance recipients. In addition, there is the particularly perverse possibility that the tenant rental contribution required of welfare recipients in all as paid states[26] who also have some income from earnings may be higher than for tenants with income only from earnings.[27] This could occur if, in addition to the welfare rent pass through, these welfare recipients were required to contribute some fraction of their earnings toward rent.[28]

The welfare rent issue highlights some of the specific ways that broader public policy goals are not being achieved by the current bifurcated system. In the absence of better coordination between housing and welfare policy and program implementation, it is difficult to see how they can be achieved.

SHELTER ASSISTANCE UNDER WELFARE: THE AGGREGATE PICTURE

The intricacies of each state's approach to shelter assistance under each of the three welfare programs provides part of the picture of the inequities in shelter subsidies across the nation. Aggregate characteristics complete the picture.

Three sets of comparisons are presented in this section. All attempt to tap the concept of relative shelter generosity. Since the number of needy individuals in each state varies widely, comparisons of absolute dollar allocations would provide a distorted view of relative generosity. Therefore, all comparisons are on a per recipient basis.[29] There are sizable disparities in shelter generosity under the three programs in many states (table 2.4). The greatest dispersion exists in Alaska, where the per capita monthly shelter allocation under SSI is $186, under AFDC is $64, and under GA is $0. Other states with large variations include Colorado, Iowa, and Minnesota. At the other extreme, Virginia, South Dakota, Utah and Kansas have per capita shelter allocations that fall within $25 of each other under the three programs. In contrast to Alaska and other states with substantial dispersion, these more uniform states also tend to have per capita allocations that fall in the lower end of the generosity range. This pattern suggests that states that are relatively more generous in one welfare program are not necessarily likely to be generous in all, although states with relatively low generosity in one or two programs are somewhat more likely to be ungenerous in all.

Contrary to expectations, relative generosity does not seem to be strongly related to the degree of federal funding. The federally matched

Table 2.4 AFDC, SSI, AND GA SHELTER ALLOCATIONS, RECIPIENTS, AND PER CAPITA ALLOCATIONS

State	AFDC			SSI			GA[b]		
	Shelter payments	Recipients	Shelter per recipient[a]	Shelter payments	Recipients	Shelter per recipient[a]	Shelter payments	Recipients	Shelter per recipient[a]
Alabama	21,887,717	154,426	12	91,798,153	127,849	60	0	0	0
Alaska	10,094,527	13,238	64	6,724,994	3,015	186	0	0	0
Arizona	22,004,852	65,579	28	26,105,056	29,236	74	1,729,030	4,313	33
Arkansas	6,354,607	63,574	8	45,351,464	71,503	53	0	0	0
California	1,052,699,682	1,514,441	58	746,153,711	653,383	95	87,547,685	71,070	103
Colorado	27,394,355	67,372	34	36,746,658	28,366	108	0	0	0
Connecticut	83,938,608	127,048	55	30,231,643	23,943	105	37,060,290	29,441	105
Delaware	7,800,003	25,400	26	5,211,812	6,893	63	2,071,360	3,633	48
District of Columbia	21,599,988	72,000	25	13,976,936	14,758	79	6,668,760	5,671	98
Florida	72,991,296	266,369	23	140,821,583	170,904	69	2,700,000	1,940	116
Georgia	55,659,027	239,363	19	103,499,982	147,945	58	1,186,451	3,750	26
Hawaii	49,230,501	50,200	82	9,176,749	9,980	77	10,841,961	8,424	107
Idaho	5,383,043	18,544	24	6,759,324	7,542	75	0	0	0
Illinois	380,186,593	730,460	43	109,681,031	119,761	76	174,413,982	146,547	99
Indiana	48,212,550	167,696	24	30,709,929	40,532	63	0	0	0
Iowa	13,184,420	111,000	10	16,816,652	25,530	55	1,465,428	1,053	116
Kansas	28,274,982	69,494	34	13,414,658	19,549	57	7,531,994	13,036	48
Kentucky	37,540,103	150,616	21	74,695,196	91,685	68	642,000	557	96
Louisiana	42,976,720	213,151	17	91,991,133	123,093	62	2,169,693	3,367	54
Maine	18,353,040	62,000	25	13,090,358	20,684	53	6,273,465	10,949	48
Maryland	94,101,048	192,448	41	39,923,341	47,197	70	17,051,212	22,161	64
Massachusetts	144,685,901	245,825	49	92,101,122	108,378	71	53,843,233	32,232	139
Michigan	328,668,463	750,914	36	102,975,368	110,542	78	245,670,275	177,584	115
Minnesota	68,925,775	146,490	39	22,890,044	29,852	64	29,658,464	16,537	149
Mississippi	12,259,207	148,482	7	76,786,987	109,063	59	0	0	0
Missouri	60,000,009	190,000	26	58,534,479	77,074	63	4,327,061	5,136	70
Montana	11,909,944	17,263	57	5,054,161	6,678	63	1,416,721	1,399	84

Table 2.4 (continued)

State	AFDC Shelter payments	AFDC Recipients	AFDC Shelter per recipient[a]	SSI Shelter payments	SSI Recipients	SSI Shelter per recipient[a]	GA[b] Shelter payments	GA[b] Recipients	GA[b] Shelter per recipient[a]
Nebraska	16,743,495	40,910	34	10,666,600	13,001	68	964,962	1,065	76
Nevada	3,415,829	13,044	22	5,524,448	6,899	67	140,756	408	29
New Hampshire	11,114,997	18,192	51	6,842,982	5,308	107	844,923	1,244	57
New Jersey	135,252,398	407,240	28	78,471,485	85,078	77	26,893,370	31,014	72
New Mexico	22,299,593	42,550	44	18,857,447	24,600	64	658,380	653	84
New York	917,242,079	1,081,264	71	327,459,917	336,463	81	389,143,116	265,723	122
North Carolina	43,621,105	169,755	21	105,049,494	131,937	66	0	0	0
North Dakota	3,685,239	10,815	28	4,285,905	5,838	61	204,379	290	59
Ohio	204,746,967	652,651	26	94,579,874	115,324	68	96,146,877	164,976	49
Oklahoma	22,957,998	69,645	27	50,364,296	59,081	71	0	0	0
Oregon	37,920,452	72,323	44	22,584,408	23,123	81	3,716,799	5,509	56
Pennsylvania	218,099,133	559,152	33	134,517,547	154,026	73	81,178,292	146,300	46
Rhode Island	20,438,569	45,282	38	11,719,495	14,482	67	6,670,062	6,149	90
South Carolina	20,496,910	133,793	13	58,283,504	81,071	60	0	0	0
South Dakota	8,809,148	16,676	44	5,207,813	7,663	57	109,630	147	62
Tennessee	24,684,378	151,399	14	89,331,733	124,149	60	0	0	0
Texas	56,952,848	302,646	16	161,298,869	244,278	55	2,769,400	5,000	46
Utah	21,062,593	36,097	49	6,058,727	7,835	64	3,238,166	3,795	71
Vermont	14,811,269	24,827	50	7,259,607	8,743	69	0	0	0
Virginia	89,657,770	160,556	47	60,567,609	79,320	64	5,716,499	10,205	47
Washington	134,339,912	158,978	70	38,678,798	43,730	74	20,038,828	13,569	123
West Virginia	16,011,334	92,894	14	33,001,700	39,571	69	0	0	0
Wisconsin	136,200,352	258,503	44	53,242,009	62,610	71	19,465,380	25,047	65
Wyoming	3,269,208	7,161	38	1,324,868	1,796	61	775,504	917	71

a. Total shelter payments for each program are divided by twelve and then divided by average monthly recipients.
b. See appendix D for assumptions underlying GA estimates. Note that since data on both recipients and cases were missing for Florida and South Dakota, we derived recipients by applying the national average of recipients to GA expenditures to each state's GA expenditures.

SSI program is the most generously funded in thirty states, but in several the level is very close to the GA shelter allocation.[30] GA programs--for which there is no federal match--have the highest per capita shelter allocations in twenty-one states. In no state is the AFDC program the most generously funded.

Relative Shelter Generosity Across States, by Program. A different perspective on intra-state variation results from shifting the base of comparison from a state's relative per capita allocations to the three programs to a comparison of its standing on each of these programs relative to other states (table 2.5). Virginia, for example, has relatively low dispersion in generosity among its three programs but greater dispersion when it is ranked relative to the other states: although its per capita budget for each program is identical for both AFDC and GA ($47), it ranks 12th under AFDC and 33rd under GA. In contrast, Hawaii, New York, Connecticut, California and Washington have consistently high rankings on all three programs; Alabama, Arizona, Mississippi, South Carolina and Tennessee have consistently low rankings.

Two findings emerge from the two perspectives on intra-state variations in the generosity of shelter allocations. First, since the most generously funded welfare programs are not uniformly those that are federally matched, concerns about such financial incentives biasing state funding decisions with regard to shelter allowances have little empirical foundation. Second, although states that have the most generous per capita shelter allocation in a particular welfare program are not very likely to be equally generous in all programs, a few states do emerge as consistently more generous across programs. New York, California and Connecticut are the three states that rank in the top 10 on shelter generosity in all three welfare programs.

The disaggregate data on the actual shelter grants paid to recipients reviewed earlier in this chapter (pp. 20-31) lead to a similar conclusion. While most of the states that have the highest ratios in one program do not have equally high ratios in the others, a few states provide actual shelter grants that are more uniformly in line with their area's FMR. This small group of states overlaps with those that have consistently high rankings and allocations in the aggregate data.

These conclusions are further supported by examining inter-state variations in shelter generosity in each of the three welfare programs. The consistency of shelter allocations in the three programs across the 51 jurisdictions is still relatively weak. But once again it is strong in a small subset of relatively generous states (California, New York and Washington). Furthermore, the relationship between funding levels is considerably stronger for AFDC and GA programs ($r = .49$) and AFDC and SSI programs ($r = .48$) than for SSI and GA programs ($r = .26$).[31]

Table 2.5   AFDC, SSI, AND GA RANKS BY PER CAPITA SHELTER ALLOCATIONS

State	AFDC shelter per recipient	SSI shelter per recipient	GA shelter per recipient
Hawaii	1	11	8
New York	2	7	4
Washington	3	15	3
Alaska	4	1	--
California	5	5	10
Montana	6	36	15
Connecticut	7	4	9
New Hampshire	8	3	26
Vermont	9	22	--
Massachusetts	10	19	2
Utah	11	30	19
Virginia	12	33	33
South Dakota	13	47	24
Wisconsin	14	18	22
Oregon	15	6	27
New Mexico	16	32	16
Illinois	17	12	11
Maryland	18	20	23
Minnesota	19	31	1
Wyoming	20	39	20
Rhode Island	21	27	14
Michigan	22	9	7
Nebraska	23	24	17
Kansas	24	46	30
Colorado	25	2	--
Pennsylvania	26	16	34
North Dakota	27	40	25
Arizona	28	14	36
New Jersey	29	10	18
Oklahoma	30	17	--
Missouri	31	34	21
Ohio	32	25	29
Delaware	33	37	32
District of Columbia	34	8	12
Maine	35	51	31
Idaho	36	13	--
Indiana	37	35	--
Florida	38	23	5
Nevada	39	28	37
North Carolina	40	29	--
Kentucky	41	26	13

Table 2.5 (continued)

State	AFDC shelter per recipient	SSI shelter per recipient	GA shelter per recipient
Georgia	42	45	38
Louisiana	43	38	28
Texas	44	48	35
West Virginia	45	21	--
Tennessee	46	41	--
South Carolina	47	42	--
Alabama	48	43	--
Iowa	49	49	6
Arkansas	50	50	--
Mississippi	51	44	--

-- Denotes no GA program.

Relative Shelter Generosity Across States, by Total Welfare Allocation. The third component of this aggregate analysis, the variation in shelter allocation for the three welfare programs taken together, is summarized in table 2.6. The first three data columns show the total welfare shelter allocations in each state, total recipients, and the resulting shelter generosity of the state's welfare system. A factor of more than two, on average, divides the shelter allocations of the most generous 10 percent of states and the least generous 10 percent. The most generous state, Alaska, provides more than four and a half times the level of shelter assistance than the least generous state, Iowa. Alaska's lead in generosity, however, is accounted for largely by its extremely small recipient population. At the other end of the continuum, Iowa has more than eight times the recipients of Alaska. It should also be noted that Alaska has no GA program; total shelter allocations, therefore, represent SSI and AFDC alone.

Table 2.7 provides another view of the variation in shelter generosity. The largest number of states falling into one shelter allocation per capita interval is seventeen (33 percent of all states), even when the interval encompasses as large a range as $100. Compressing the interval, of course, yields more dramatic results: the largest number of states with shelter allocations per capita within $25 of each other is eight.[32]

The final two columns of table 2.6 rank states by the number of welfare recipients and welfare shelter generosity. California and New York are the only two states that rank high in terms of both recipients and generosity. Alaska, for example, is the most generous state overall, but ranks fiftieth in number of recipients. At other points in

Table 2.6 VARIATION IN TOTAL WELFARE SHELTER ALLOCATION GENEROSITY

State	Total shelter payments	Total recipients per month	Annual shelter payments per recipient	Rank by number of recipients	Rank by shelter payment per recipient
California	1,886,401,077	2,238,894	843	1	5
New York	1,633,845,113	1,683,450	971	2	3
Michigan	677,314,107	1,039,040	652	3	13
Illinois	664,281,606	996,768	666	4	11
Ohio	395,473,719	932,951	424	5	38
Pennsylvania	433,794,972	859,478	505	6	26
Texas	221,021,116	551,924	400	7	45
New Jersey	240,617,254	523,332	460	8	34
Florida	216,512,879	439,213	493	9	28
Georgia	160,345,460	391,058	410	10	41
Massachusetts	290,630,256	386,435	752	11	8
Wisconsin	208,907,741	346,160	604	12	19
Louisiana	137,137,546	339,611	404	13	42
North Carolina	148,670,599	301,692	493	14	29
Alabama	113,685,870	282,275	403	15	44
Tennessee	114,016,111	275,548	414	16	40
Missouri	122,861,549	272,210	451	17	36
Maryland	151,075,600	261,806	577	18	21
Mississippi	89,046,194	257,545	346	19	50
Virginia	155,941,879	250,081	624	20	17
Kentucky	112,877,299	242,858	465	21	33
Washington	193,057,538	216,277	893	22	4
South Carolina	78,780,414	214,864	367	23	49
Indiana	78,922,479	208,228	379	24	47

Table 2.6 (continued)

State	Total shelter payments	Total recipients per month	Annual shelter payments per recipient	Rank by number of recipients	Rank by shelter payment per recipient
Minnesota	121,474,283	192,879	630	25	16
Connecticut	151,230,542	180,432	838	26	6
Iowa	31,466,499	137,583	229	27	51
Arkansas	51,706,071	135,077	383	28	46
West Virginia	49,013,034	132,465	370	29	48
Oklahoma	73,322,294	128,726	570	30	23
Kansas	49,221,635	102,079	482	31	31
Oregon	64,221,658	100,955	636	32	14
Arizona	49,838,938	99,128	503	33	27
Colorado	64,141,014	95,738	670	34	10
Maine	37,716,862	93,633	403	35	43
District of Columbia	42,245,684	92,429	457	36	35
Hawaii	69,249,211	68,604	1,009	37	2
New Mexico	41,815,420	67,803	617	38	18
Rhode Island	38,828,126	65,913	589	39	20
Nebraska	28,375,057	54,976	516	40	25
Utah	30,359,486	47,727	636	41	15
Delaware	15,083,175	35,926	420	42	39
Vermont	22,070,876	33,570	657	43	12
Idaho	12,142,367	26,086	465	44	32
Montana	18,380,827	25,340	725	45	9
New Hampshire	18,802,902	24,744	760	46	7
South Dakota	14,126,590	24,486	577	47	22
Nevada	9,081,032	20,351	446	48	37
North Dakota	8,175,523	16,943	483	49	30
Alaska	16,819,521	16,253	1,035	50	1
Wyoming	5,369,580	9,874	544	51	24

Table 2.7 SIZE AND RANK OF STATES BY TOTAL POPULATION, POPULATION IN POVERTY AND TOTAL WELFARE SHELTER ALLOCATIONS

State	1980 population	Rank by population	1980 population in poverty	Rank by population in poverty	Total shelter payments (dollars)	Rank by total shelter payments
California	23,677,902	1	2,626,600	1	1,886,401,077	1
New York	17,558,072	2	2,298,900	2	1,633,845,113	2
Texas	14,229,191	3	2,035,900	3	221,021,116	9
Florida	9,746,324	7	1,287,100	4	216,512,879	10
Illinois	11,426,518	5	1,230,500	5	644,281,606	4
Pennsylvania	11,863,895	4	1,209,800	6	433,794,972	5
Ohio	10,797,630	6	1,089,000	7	395,473,710	6
Michigan	9,262,078	8	945,900	8	677,314,107	3
Georgia	5,463,105	13	884,400	9	160,345,460	13
North Carolina	5,881,766	10	839,900	10	148,670,599	17
Louisiana	4,205,900	19	764,800	11	137,137,546	18
Tennessee	4,591,120	17	736,500	12	114,016,111	21
Alabama	3,893,888	22	719,900	13	113,685,870	22
New Jersey	7,364,823	9	689,500	14	240,617,254	8
Kentucky	3,660,777	23	626,200	15	112,877,299	23
Virginia	5,346,818	14	611,300	16	155,941,879	14
Mississippi	2,520,638	31	587,400	17	89,046,194	24
Missouri	4,916,686	15	582,300	18	122,861,549	19
Massachusetts	5,737,037	11	532,500	19	290,630,256	7
Indiana	5,490,224	12	516,200	20	78,922,479	25
South Carolina	3,121,820	24	500,400	21	78,780,414	26
Arkansas	2,286,435	33	423,600	22	51,706,071	31
Maryland	4,216,975	18	404,600	23	151,075,600	16
Wisconsin	4,705,767	16	397,800	24	208,907,741	11
Washington	4,132,156	20	395,600	25	193,057,538	12
Oklahoma	3,025,290	26	393,900	26	73,322,294	27

Table 2.7 (continued)

State	1980 population	Rank by population	1980 population in poverty	Rank by population in poverty	Total shelter payments (dollars)	Rank by total shelter payments
Minnesota	4,075,950	21	375,000	27	121,474,283	20
Arizona	2,718,215	29	351,400	28	49,838,938	32
West Virginia	1,949,644	34	287,000	29	49,013,934	34
Iowa	2,913,808	27	286,200	30	31,466,499	39
Colorado	2,889,964	28	284,900	31	64,141,014	30
Oregon	2,633,105	30	274,200	32	64,221,658	29
Connecticut	3,107,576	25	242,600	33	151,230,542	15
Kansas	2,363,679	32	231,700	34	49,221,635	33
New Mexico	1,302,894	37	225,500	35	41,815,420	36
Nebraska	1,569,825	35	163,300	36	28,375,057	41
Utah	1,461,037	36	148,000	37	30,359,486	40
Maine	1,124,660	38	141,000	38	37,716,862	38
Idaho	943,935	41	116,800	39	12,142,367	48
District of Columbia	638,333	47	113,400	40	42,245,684	35
South Dakota	690,768	45	112,700	41	14,126,590	47
Montana	786,690	44	94,300	42	18,380,827	44
Rhode Island	947,154	40	94,000	43	38,828,126	37
Hawaii	964,691	39	91,600	44	69,249,211	28
North Dakota	652,717	46	79,300	45	8,175,523	50
New Hampshire	920,610	42	75,400	46	18,802,902	43
Nevada	800,493	43	68,700	47	9,081,032	49
Delaware	594,338	48	68,400	48	15,083,175	46
Vermont	511,456	49	59,100	49	22,070,876	42
Alaska	401,851	51	41,600	50	16,819,521	45
Wyoming	469,557	50	36,300	51	5,369,580	51

the continuum, very few states have similar rankings on both dimensions; these include Massachusetts, Maryland, Virginia, the District of Columbia, and Kansas (which ranks thirty-first on both recipients and generosity). There clearly is no relationship between the size of the recipient population and shelter allocation generosity.

It is noteworthy, however, that the ten states with the largest poverty populations in the country (accounting for more than 50 percent of the nation's poor) also rank among the top states in total welfare shelter allocations. Among these consistently high ranking states are California, New York, Illinois, Pennsylvania, Ohio and Michigan. These patterns are shown in figure 2.1.[33] While the size of the poverty population in these states is larger than that in other states, their ratios of poverty to non-poverty population are about at the mean. Interpreting this ratio as a measure of fiscal dependence provides some insight into the variation in state funding decisions. The fact that Mississippi, for example, ranks roughly in the middle of the distribution on shelter allocations rather than at the top may have as much to do with the fact that its fiscal dependency ratio is more than two times the average ratio as with its "taste" for redistribution.[34,35]

SUMMARY

The current system of shelter assistance inherent in general welfare programs almost guarantees major horizontal inequities (i.e., that similar individuals living in different locations in the U.S. will not be treated similarly). Depending on whether shelter subsidies are explicit or embedded in a consolidated grant, whether they are based on a realistic need standard that is updated regularly and funded fully, whether they are adjusted for such variables as family size and high versus low cost areas within the jurisdiction, recipients will either receive shelter payments that afford them decent housing or not. On average, neither AFDC, SSI nor GA provides shelter payments that equal even the lowest FMRs as shown in the last three columns of table 2.8.

Vertical equity (that is, the appropriate treatment of different groups of needy individuals) fares no better. Overall, SSI recipients, predominantly the poor elderly, are treated more consistently and generously than GA and AFDC recipients. While there is some variation between these programs' shelter payment levels in the Northeast and North Central regions, the main source of variation lies in the South, where SSI funds nearly two-thirds of the FMR but AFDC and GA fund only one-quarter and one-third, respectively.

Figure 2.1 DISTRIBUTION OF WELFARE SHELTER ALLOCATIONS
PER RECIPIENT

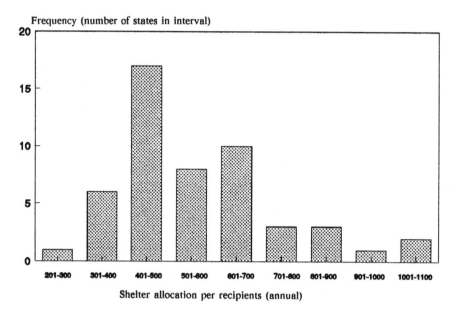

Frequency (number of states in interval)

Shelter allocation per recipients (annual)

With the exception of a handful of states, states that generously fund shelter subsidies in one welfare program are not more likely to generously fund them in all.[36] There is a somewhat clearer pattern of consistency among ungenerous states: at the lower end of the funding continuum, states providing less generous shelter allocations in one or two programs appear somewhat more likely to provide uniformly low allocations in all three programs.

In the face of so much dispersion at the upper end of shelter funding and greater uniformity only at the lower end, the few states that emerge as consistently generous are all the more impressive. Among these, California and New York are particularly noteworthy as they are also the states with the largest recipient populations. Since these states' fiscal dependency ratios (i.e., the ratio of the poverty population to the non-poverty population) are no lower than the mean for all states, it can be argued that their higher shelter allocations are a reasonable reflection of their generosity. In contrast, generosity may have less to do with the low shelter allocations of Arkansas and Mississippi, for example, which have fiscal dependency ratios that are much higher than average.

Table 2.8 COMPARISON OF SHELTER PAYMENT UNDER AFDC, SSI, AND GA, 1984-85 DATA

Region	AFDC shelter payment, four-person family	FMR, two-bedroom unit	SSI shelter payment, single-person household	FMR, zero-bedroom	GA shelter payment single-person household	AFDC shelter payment, FMR (percent)	SSI shelter payment, FMR (percent)	GA shelter payment, FMR (percent)
Northeast	178	301	144	208	149	59.0	69.0	77.0
North Central	138	266	117	180	111	52.0	65.0	62.0
South	76	278	109	180	76	27.0	61.0	34.0
West	208	326	157	236	145	64.0	67.0	60.0
Weighted average	144	289	127	198	129	50.0	64.0	68.0

Notes:
(1) AFDC shelter payment calculations assume national distribution of family size for each state.
(2) Regional and national AFDC averages were computed by weighting each state's shelter payment and shelter payment to FMR ratio by the state's average monthly caseload.
(3) Regional and national SSI averages were computed by weighting each state's shelter payment and shelter payment to FMR ratio by the state's total caseload.
(4) SSI shelter payment and shelter payment to FMR ratio calculations use method II described in text which combines the 33 percent reduction in the federal payment with the specific adjustment made by each state that provided supplementary SSI payments.
(5) Regional and national GA averages were computed by weighting each state's shelter payment and shelter payment to FMR ratio by the state's average monthly recipients.

Notes

1. These states are: Hawaii, Idaho, Indiana, Michigan, New Hampshire, New York, Oregon, South Dakota and Vermont. In recent months, Michigan and South Dakota have decided to discontinue their explicit payment approach. Our data, however, reflect the 1984-5 period when they were still applying this method.

2. This rate was also adopted by Nenno (4).

3. The FMR is the accepted measure of the cost of minimally adequate housing in the nation's housing markets. FMRs are developed through quantitative analysis of decennial census, America Housing Survey, and Consumer Price Index data. Although the FMR system has weaknesses as well as strengths--a characterization that applies to the official poverty line, HUD's housing quality standards, and almost any other standard--it is the most readily available yardstick by which to judge the cost of decent housing.

4. The average AFDC family size is roughly three persons (5).

5. Alabama, Arkansas, Mississippi, Nevada, South Carolina, Tennessee, and West Virginia.

6. We restrict our attention to this segment of the SSI program and exclude consideration of special housing settings and recipients.

7. This method should result in an upper bound value since the one-third value covers the full range of "support and maintenance in-kind," thereby including other support than just shelter.

8. The three states with explicit shelter payments are excluded from these counts.

9. In two cases, payments to individuals living alone versus with (nonspouse) others are treated differently from payments to couples.

10. The differences between the two methods of extracting shelter payments under SSI are negligible except in the Northeast, where the discrepancy in shelter payment to FMR ratios is 7 percentage points. This discrepancy is due almost entirely to the state of Connecticut, which has a shelter maximum of $200 (under method II) compared to its one-third estimate of $155 (method I).

11. In fiscal 1984, two states--Alabama and West Virginia--had essentially no income assistance available for GA-type populations. In another eleven states (Alaska, Arkansas, Colorado, Idaho, Indiana, Mississippi, North Carolina, Oklahoma, South Carolina, Tennessee and Vermont) only short-term or one-time emergency assistance was available.

12. These twenty states are: Arizona, Delaware, District of Columbia, Hawaii, Illinois, Kansas, Maryland, Massachusetts, Michigan, Minnesota, Missouri, New Jersey, New Mexico, New York, Ohio, Oregon, Pennsylvania, Utah, Washington, and Wyoming.

13. The trend toward consolidation, however, is clear: several states, including Illinois and Minnesota, moved to consolidated payments in the early 1980s and a number of other states, such as Ohio, are seriously considering consolidation.

14. Louisiana, Missouri, New Jersey, Rhode Island, and South Dakota. The national average was weighted by recipients per state. We chose the national rather than regional average because of the great amount of intra-regional variation.

15. Table 2.3 includes thirty-seven of the thirty-eight states with GA programs. New Hampshire has been deleted because of insufficient data.

16. These states are: Connecticut, Georgia, Michigan, Minnesota, Oregon, and Washington.

17. Arizona, Delaware, Maryland, Nevada, South Dakota, and Wyoming.

18. According to HUD regulations (24 CFR Section 913), the treatment of welfare recipients in states with explicit shelter payments as described is this section could apply to any welfare program that provides explicit grants for shelter. To date, these procedures have only been applied to AFDC and, to a very limited extent, to General Assistance.

19. At present, this situation occurs in two states: Idaho and Indiana. AFDC recipients in these states account for roughly 2 percent of all AFDC recipients in the nation in a typical month. (See table 2.4.)

20. Gross income minus expenditures for necessities such as medical care.

21. The procedures are roughly as follows. State X establishes $100 as its shelter need standard. In addition, because of state budget constraints, it sets 50 percent as its ratable reduction. HUD applies this ratable reduction to the need standard and establishes $50 as the tenant's rent contribution. State X then interprets this $50 as the measure of the tenant's actual rent. Since it is the actual rent that is required to be ratably reduced in order to derive the actual shelter payment, the state applies the 50 percent to the $50. The tenant's actual shelter grant is, therefore, $25, even though HUD has set its rent contribution at $50. (See White v. Pierce, 1986.)

22. PHAs are the main administrative agencies for assisted housing.

23. Smith v. Pierce (Vermont, 1982); Howard v. Pierce (Michigan, 1982); White v. Pierce (Idaho, 1983).

24. For example, if the maximum rent payment a state will make under its welfare program is $142, under current HUD regulations HUD would calculate a tenant's rental contribution as $142 x .55 = $78. The public welfare agency would set the shelter payment at $42, leaving $36 to be made up by the tenant. If the tenant were not in assisted housing, however, the amount to be made up would be $64, the difference between $78 (the shelter payment) and $142 (the actual rent).

25. The absolute dollar value of the shelter payment in as paid states may be lower than the absolute dollar value of non-welfare housing assistance recipients' payments, but the housing cost to income ratios are very likely to be considerably higher than 30 percent.

26. Recipients in as paid states account for nearly 22 percent of all AFDC recipients in an average month. (See table 2.4.)

27. Recent evidence from the Panel Study of Income Dynamics indicates that about 10 percent of female heads of households receiving welfare also receive some labor income at the same time (7).

28. This issue has not been addressed at the federal level (8).

29. This procedure introduces some bias of its own, since it assumes that the average recipients in a month are likely to remain recipients over the full year (i.e., average monthly recipients equal average annual recipients). This is unlikely to be the case, particularly for GA. However, since this bias should be consistent across all states and we are interested in relative rather than absolute values, we believe it will not distort the main results.

30. In thirteen of the thirty states there is no GA program at all.

31. Pearson correlation coefficients.

32. These eight states fall within the shelter allocation per capita interval of $400 to $424. In addition to these eight states, three groups of six states each also fall within $25 of each other. The intervals for these groups are $482 to $505, $446 to $465, and $379 to $404, respectively.

33. Pennsylvania and Ohio rank consistently highly here but not on recipients and per capita allocations because, although they have a large pool of recipients, their per capita allocations are below the median.

34. The average ratio of the poverty to non-poverty population in the U.S. in 1980 was about .14.

35. Another indicator of generosity is the restrictiveness of eligibility rules for participation in welfare programs. One way to measure this concept is to look at the ratio of recipients to the total poverty population. Unfortunately, we have no way to estimate this precisely since our recipient data are for 1984 while the poverty population estimates are for 1980. On the assumption of no major shifts among states in the intervening years, these ratios can provide some insight into the relative standing of states. Mississippi's ratio is roughly in the middle of the distribution; those for California and New York are, again, at the top.

36. As an aside, since there is no tendency for the more generously funded programs to be those for which federal matching dollars are available, there is also no basis for concern that the presence of a federal match has a non-neutral effect on state funding decisions.

3

THE IMPACT OF THE TWO-PRONGED SYSTEM

This chapter examines the impact of the two-pronged system for subsidizing housing on the housing situation of program recipients. Several key questions are addressed:

o What is the magnitude and nature of the overlap between housing assistance and income assistance programs?

o What kinds of households receive various combinations of income and housing aid?

o How do housing conditions vary according to types of subsidies received?

o How is the housing situation of the welfare population related to the size of their shelter allowance?

Answers to these questions will enable us to assess the current system in terms of its equity, its efficiency, and its overall effectiveness in serving the housing needs of the nation's poor.

DATA SOURCES

The analysis relies on two different data sets. The first, and most important, is the national file of the 1983 American Housing Survey (AHS). This survey was administered to over 90,000 households across the country, and provides detailed information on the characteristics of both the household and its dwelling unit.

We also use data obtained from the metropolitan files of the 1982 and 1983 AHS, which provide information on housing conditions and costs in 25 different SMSAs. These files are similar in content to the national AHS, but focus on particular sites. Since the sample size in a given SMSA is relatively large (about 3,500 observations), this second data set enables us to relate the housing conditions of the welfare population to the specific shelter allowance that they receive (based on the state survey data described in chapter 2).

Both AHS data sets identify households with income from "welfare payments or other public assistance," including AFDC, SSI, GA, and a host of other smaller welfare programs (e.g., refugee aid, emergency assistance). They also identify households in public housing projects or in units which have reduced rents "because the federal, state, or local government is paying part of the cost." While owner-occupants with subsidized mortgages are not identified, the size of such programs (e.g., Section 235) is relatively small. As a result, the data provide reasonably good estimates of the overlap between income assistance and housing aid.

THE OVERLAP BETWEEN HOUSING AND INCOME ASSISTANCE

In 1983,[1] almost 8 million households (or 9 percent of all U.S. households) were receiving some form of housing or income assistance (table 3.1). About 4.6 million households were receiving income assistance alone; about 2.1 million were receiving housing subsidies, but not income assistance; about 1.3 million were receiving both types of aid.

The majority of participants receive only one form of subsidy. However, about 22 percent of the welfare population also receives a direct housing subsidy,[2] and about 38 percent of all households currently receiving a housing subsidy are also receiving income assistance.

GEOGRAPHIC DISTRIBUTION

The Northeast and the South have the highest concentration of households receiving housing subsidies (table 3.2). The South also has the highest share of households with income assistance. However, regional variations in the distribution of households with income assistance are relatively small, and tend to reflect differences in the distribution of the poverty population at large.

Table 3.1   BREAKDOWN OF HOUSEHOLDS BY TYPE OF ASSISTANCE, 1983

Households	Number of households (thousands)	Percent renters[a]
Receiving income assistance	5,864	70.0
Receiving housing assistance	3,392	100.0
Type of assistance		
Income assistance only	4,568	61.0
Housing assistance only	2,096	100.0
Income and housing assistance	1,296	100.0
Income and/or housing assistance	7,960[b]	

Source: The 1983 National American Housing Survey.

a. Includes households that neither own nor rent
b. Total unweighted number of cases = 5,307.

Housing subsidies tend to be more concentrated in larger urban areas than is income assistance. Forty-four percent of all households with housing assistance live in the central cities of larger SMSAs; the comparable figure for households on welfare is 36 percent. Similarly, only 23 percent of all households with housing assistance live in non-metropolitan areas, compared to 32 percent of those on welfare. This geographic tilt of housing subsidies towards urban areas is particularly evident among households receiving both income and housing assistance. Forty-eight percent of all such households live in the central cities of larger SMSAs.

An alternative way to view the geographic distribution by subsidy type is to consider the proportion of households with income assistance who also receive a housing subsidy. This proportion ranges from 15 percent in non-metropolitan areas to about 29 percent in the central cities of large SMSAs. Most of this difference arises because the proportion of the welfare population that rents is much higher in central cities (77 percent) than it is in non-metropolitan areas (42 percent). Among renters with income assistance, the proportion receiving a housing subsidy is about the same in the central cities of large SMSAs (38 percent) as it is in non-metropolitan areas (36 percent).

Table 3.2 DISTRIBUTION OF ASSISTED HOUSEHOLDS BY LOCATION, 1983 (percent)

Region	Receiving income assistance	Receiving housing assistance	Type of assistance		
			Income assistance only	Housing assistance only	Income and housing assistance
Northeast	23.5	30.0	22.4	31.7	27.3
North Central	25.7	22.7	26.3	22.2	23.6
South	29.9	30.0	30.5	31.3	27.8
West	20.9	17.3	20.7	14.9	21.2
	100.0	100.0	100.0	100.0	100.0
Large SMSAs					
Central city	36.2	43.8	32.8	41.2	48.1
Suburban ring	18.2	18.2	19.2	20.3	14.8
Small SMSAs	13.9	15.1	13.4	14.8	15.6
Non-metropolitan	31.7	22.9	34.6	23.7	21.5
	100.0	100.0	100.0	100.0	100.0
Memorandum item					
Sample size	3,918	1,966	3,187	1,235	731

THE DEMOGRAPHIC CHARACTERISTICS OF RECIPIENTS

In general, households receiving both income and housing assistance have significantly lower incomes, higher concentrations of minorities and higher proportions of female-headed households with children than the recipient population as a whole (table 3.3). Such households tend to be larger than those with housing assistance alone; but they are substantially smaller than the average welfare-only household.

Many of the differences between multiple and single subsidy households are quite pronounced. For example, 64 percent of the households with combined subsidies have incomes that are less than $5,000 per year, compared to 40 percent of households with income assistance alone, and 29 percent of households with housing assistance alone. Average family income by subsidy type ranges from $5,138 for households with income and housing assistance, to $9,109 for households with only a housing subsidy, to $9,571 for households with income assistance alone. Multiple subsidies are thus clearly targeted to the most needy segment of the population.

Another characteristic that distinguishes welfare and housing assistance recipients from one another and from the unassisted population is residential mobility.[3] The mobility rates of U.S. households and various subgroups of the poor and non-poor are shown in table 3.4. Poverty households have a mobility rate that is 50 percent greater than that of all households and 70 percent greater than households with incomes at 150 percent of poverty or more. Thus, mobility rates fall as income rises. Within the assisted population (the majority of whom are poor), the disparity in mobility rates between types of assistance is much smaller. Not surprisingly, those receiving housing assistance only are less likely to move compared to those receiving income assistance. In addition, most of the moves by housing assistance households appear to represent the initial move out of the unassisted stock into assisted units. A much smaller fraction represent shifts within the assisted stock.

What is surprising is that those receiving both welfare and housing assistance have the highest rates of mobility: 27.6 percent. The higher overall mobility rate of this group also includes a somewhat higher rate of relocation within the assisted stock than other housing assistance recipients. The higher total rate is probably related to the fact that these households are also the poorest of the three groups and much more likely to be headed by a female. Relative to other demographic groups such as the elderly, these households experience a greater frequency of life events and disruptions (e.g., changes in family size and economic instability) which are known to be related to moving.

Table 3.3 CHARACTERISTICS OF HOUSEHOLDS BY TYPE OF ASSISTANCE, 1983 (percent)

Characteristic	Receiving income assistance	Receiving housing assistance	Type of assistance		
			Income assistance only	Housing assistance only	Income and housing assistance
Household size					
One person	22.9	41.0	19.6	44.8	34.8
Two persons	21.0	21.5	21.5	23.0	19.1
Three persons	19.3	14.6	19.5	12.2	18.5
Four persons	15.9	12.1	16.8	11.6	12.7
Five plus persons	20.9	10.9	22.6	8.4	14.8
Age of head					
Under 20 years	1.5	1.0	1.5	0.5	1.7
20 to 29 years	23.7	19.7	23.3	16.3	25.3
30 to 49 years	32.9	28.4	33.6	27.1	30.6
50 to 61 years	16.3	12.6	16.4	10.6	15.9
62 plus years	25.6	38.3	25.3	45.6	26.7
	100.0	100.0	100.0	100.0	100.0
Race/ethnicity					
White[a]	52.0	51.7	55.3	58.7	40.4
Black[a]	32.4	34.6	29.4	29.4	43.0
Hispanic	12.5	10.5	12.0	8.3	14.1
Other[a]	3.2	3.2	3.4	3.6	2.5
	100.0	100.0	100.0	100.0	100.0

Table 3.3 (continued)

Characteristic	Receiving income assistance	Receiving housing assistance	Type of assistance		
			Income assistance only	Housing assistance only	Income and housing assistance
Mean family income (dollars)	8,592	7,592	9,571	9,109	5,138
Household type					
Elderly (65+)					
Single-person	12.0	27.9	9.9	33.1	19.4
Other	10.0	6.6	11.7	8.3	3.9
Non-elderly					
Single-person	10.9	13.1	9.7	11.7	15.5
Female-headed with children	32.1	27.6	29.0	18.1	43.0
Male-headed with children	16.2	12.8	18.3	15.3	8.8
Other	18.8	12.0	16.7	13.6	9.5
	100.0	100.0	100.0	100.0	100.0

a. Excludes households that classify themselves as Hispanic.

Table 3.4 ANNUAL RESIDENTIAL MOBILITY RATES BY POVERTY STATUS, TYPE OF ASSISTANCE AND TYPE OF WELFARE, 1983

Mobility rates	Percent of households that moved
U.S. mobility rate	17.5
Mobility rate, by poverty status	
At or below poverty	26.4
Up to 150 percent of poverty	17.8
More than 150 percent of poverty	15.5
Mobility rate, by type of assistance	
Unassisted	16.6
Income only	26.9
Housing only	23.2
Income and housing	27.6
Mobility rate, by type of welfare	
AFDC only	39.2
SSI only	10.3
GA only	31.9

In fact, the low mobility rates of the elderly are demonstrated by the data for households receiving different types of income assistance; SSI recipients, most of whom are elderly, have a very low incidence of mobility. AFDC recipients, in contrast, have a very high rate, with nearly four in ten having moved in the last year. The rate for GA recipients, 31.9 percent, is also quite high--it is 80 percent greater than that for all U.S. households.

The higher probability of welfare households being evicted is one explanation that has often been given to account for their high rates of mobility. Reasons for eviction, however, run the gamut from problems with tenants (e.g., non-payment of rent, disruptive behavior) to problems with landlords (e.g., discrimination). While the AHS interview cannot be expected to elicit valid information at this level of detail and sensitivity, the data do suggest a substantial disparity in the incidence of the more general category of "displacement" moves among welfare versus housing assistance recipients. Roughly 6 percent of households receiving income assistance only moved because they were displaced by private action.[4] This rate compares with roughly 3.1 percent for those receiving housing assistance.

Other evidence suggests that income assistance households may be particularly at risk for displacement. An analysis of urban movers during the 1970s estimated that more than one-third of all displaced households were recipients of public assistance--a rate that is substantially higher than among those who are not displaced (9).

Even though welfare households are at a greater overall risk of having to move involuntarily, the main reasons for welfare recipients to move, as for other segments of the population, relate to consumption decisions (e.g., change in family size or composition), housing or neighborhood concerns (e.g., crime, desire for better housing) or employment (e.g., looking for work), in descending order of importance.

The AHS data do not directly address the question of interstate differences in welfare payments as precipitants of mobility. The indirect evidence that can be gleaned from the single item on the location of the previous residence, however, suggests that such motivations are unlikely to play a major role in accounting for the high incidence of moving among welfare households. More than 90 percent of all welfare households who moved remained in the same state. As described in chapter 2, the majority of both AFDC and SSI programs have uniform payments within states.

The final set of policy questions focus on the effects of moving on welfare households and, in particular, on housing outcomes. A comparison of the attributes of pre- and post-move residences of welfare households indicate that, in terms of dwelling quality, these households appear to be better off after they move. This finding is wholly consistent with the data reported earlier indicating that consumption and housing-related reasons represent the main motivations for changing residence. Their rate of crowding declined by 47 percent, from 23 percent before moving to 15.6 percent after the move.[5] In addition, they experienced some decline in the rate of structural deficiencies in their dwellings: the fraction sharing or lacking complete plumbing, for example, declined by about one-fourth (from 7 percent to 5.6 percent).

These improvements in quality appear to be gained at some expense. Among renters, for example, the fraction with gross rents of $150 per month or less declines by nearly half (from 15.4 percent to 8.4 percent).[6] The resultant shift in the rent distribution, however, is toward the middle of the range (i.e., rents of roughly $250-$300); the proportion of movers paying rents of $300 or more pre- and post-move remains essentially the same (roughly 38 percent).

HOUSING OUTCOMES BY TYPE OF ASSISTANCE

HUD programs establish the maximum rent-to-income ratio (including a utility allowance) at roughly 30 percent. Although some observers have argued that utility payments in excess of HUD's budgeted amounts often lead to rent burdens that are above this theoretical maximum, the ratio expected under housing programs should not be much higher than 30 percent. In contrast, given the size of the welfare grant relative to the cost of housing, housing cost-to-income ratios among welfare households are likely to be very high.

These expectations are for the most part supported by the AHS data (table 3.5). The housing costs of households in assisted housing programs ($185/month) are about 32 percent below the average costs of those receiving welfare assistance alone ($273). As a result, housing cost-to-income ratios are relatively low among households that receive a housing subsidy (36 percent). In contrast, households on welfare alone spend an average of just over half their incomes on housing. Two-thirds of all such households spend more than 30 percent, and 46 percent spend over half. Affordability is thus a major problem for this segment of the population.

It should be noted, however, that even with housing assistance a substantial proportion of households report rents that exceed the 30 percent affordability standard implicit in federal housing programs. For example, 34 percent of households receiving only a housing subsidy spend more than 30 percent of their incomes on rent, and 14 percent spend more than half. Most strikingly, some 49 percent of households with both housing and income assistance spend in excess of 30 percent of their income on housing, and 29 percent spending 50 percent or more. Some of these cases may well reflect differences in affordability standards in state or local housing programs, as well as inaccuracies in the data (due, for example, to an under-reporting of household income). However, given the relative poverty of households with multiple subsidies, inadequate utility allowances are almost certainly some of the explanation.[7]

Table 3.6 presents additional information on the extent of crowding and the physical condition of dwelling units occupied by the various groups. Units have been classified as substandard if they fail to meet housing quality standards similar to those used by HUD to define adequate housing.[8] It should be noted that this definition is only one of several in the literature and yields mid-range estimates of the incidence of substandard housing.[9] Similarly, units have been classified as crowded if they have more than one person per room. Although HUD occupancy standards often allow for a higher number of persons per room, this cut-off remains an accepted measure of crowding among different household types.

Households in subsidized housing have a relatively low incidence of substandard dwellings, and most of the defects observed reflect building maintenance as opposed to structural problems. Again, this finding is

Table 3.5 HOUSING COSTS AND AFFORDABILITY BY TYPE OF ASSISTANCE, 1983

Housing Costs	Receiving income assistance	Receiving housing assistance	Type of assistance		
			Income assistance only	Housing assistance only	Income and housing assistance
Monthly housing costs (dollars)	246	185	273	200	161
Average housing cost-to-income ratio	0.488	0.358	0.509	0.319	0.420
Housing cost-to-income ratio (distribution)					
Under 0.25	28.6	42.5	26.1	46.2	36.6
0.25 to 0.30	8.8	17.8	7.0	19.8	14.6
0.31 to 0.40	11.4	13.3	11.1	13.9	12.4
0.41 to 0.50	9.6	6.7	10.3	6.4	7.4
0.50 plus	41.6	19.6	45.5	13.7	29.0
	100.0	100.0	100.0	100.0	100.0
Paying over 30 percent	62.6	39.6	66.8	34.0	48.7

Table 3.6 ASSISTED HOUSEHOLDS BY HOUSING CONDITIONS AND TYPE OF ASSISTANCE, 1983 (percent)

Housing condition	Type of assistance				
	Receiving income assistance	Receiving housing assistance	Income assistance only	Housing assistance only	Income and housing assistance
Percent substandard	24.8	8.0	28.5	5.8	11.7
Fail major (i.e., structural problems)	7.4	0.8	9.3	0.7	0.9
Fail minor (i.e., maintenance problems)	21.9	7.4	25.0	5.1	11.1
Fail both	4.6	0.2	5.9	0.1	0.3
Persons per room (average)	0.710	0.627	0.719	0.594	0.680
Persons per room (distribution)					
Under 1.1	87.9	93.8	86.7	94.8	92.3
1.1 to 1.5	9.0	5.3	9.8	4.6	6.3
1.6 to 2.0	2.3	0.7	2.6	0.4	1.2
2.1 and over	0.8	0.2	0.9	0.2	0.1
	100.0	100.0	100.0	100.0	100.0

not surprising given that most of HUD's programs incorporate fairly stringent construction or maintenance standards that attempt to insure decent and sanitary housing conditions for program recipients.[10]

The incidence of substandard dwellings is considerably higher among the welfare only population, and major defects are much more prevalent. Nevertheless, the proportion of welfare only households in substandard units (29 percent) is less than half the proportion that pay more than 30 percent of their income for housing (67 percent). Thus, the problem of affordability appears to dominate the problem of housing quality regardless of the mix of subsidies received. Much the same conclusion can be drawn with respect to crowding, which appears to be more related to household size than to subsidy mix. While the incidence of crowding is again highest among the welfare only population, most of the crowded units still have less than 1.5 persons per room.

Table 3.7 presents information on the incidence of multiple housing problems across the different household types. Three types of problems are considered: (1) affordability (i.e., whether the household pays more than 30 percent of its income on housing); (2) crowding (i.e., whether the dwelling has more than one person per room); and (3) physical condition (i.e., whether the dwelling is classified as substandard). As is evident from the chart, a relatively large proportion of assisted households have a housing problem, regardless of the type of assistance received. However, affordability is the *only* problem for at least half of those with a housing need. The incidence of multiple deficiencies is relatively low among those in assisted housing, but the incidence is fairly high among welfare households. About 78 percent of all welfare only households have some kind of housing problem and about 23 percent have at least two.

VARIATIONS BY REGION

Chapter 2 described the geographic inequities that arise under AFDC, General Assistance, and to some extent, SSI. In particular, it documented the extremely low payment standards in the South relative to the estimated cost of standard housing. This regional variation in income assistance contrasts with the major housing assistance programs, which attempt to gear payment standards and subsidy levels to variations in market conditions and local costs. Given this basic difference in program design, one might expect the housing situations of welfare only households to differ more by region than the housing situation of households enrolled in traditional housing programs.

This expectation is at least partially confirmed (table 3.8). Despite the extremely low payment standards in the South, the proportion of

Table 3.7 ASSISTED HOUSEHOLDS BY NUMBER AND TYPE OF PROBLEM, 1983 (percent)

Region	Receiving income assistance	Receiving housing assistance	Type of assistance		
			Income assistance only	Housing assistance only	Income and housing assistance
One problem					
Crowded	3.6	3.5	3.8	3.9	2.8
Substandard	8.6	3.7	10.0	3.5	3.9
Unaffordable	40.5	33.7	41.2	31.0	38.1
Two problems	18.2	5.9	20.4	3.1	10.6
Three problems	2.4	0.4	2.9	0.2	0.7
Households with housing problems	73.3	47.2	78.2	41.6	56.1

Table 3.8 HOUSING PROBLEMS BY TYPE OF ASSISTANCE AND
GEOGRAPHIC REGION, 1983 (percent)

| Housing problem | Income assistance only | | Housing assistance only | Income and housing assistance |
	Owners	Renters		
Paying over 30 percent of income on housing				
Northeast	53.6	84.1	30.6	59.7
North Central	55.9	84.4	37.4	53.4
South	40.4	72.4	35.4	43.1
West	42.3	77.7	33.3	36.9
Paying over 50 percent				
Northeast	34.4	61.4	13.2	37.3
North Central	36.6	63.2	14.7	31.3
South	23.6	45.8	15.4	25.1
West	20.1	53.4	9.9	20.8
Substandard				
Northeast	16.6	32.3	6.1	17.6
North Central	15.0	18.7	5.9	8.3
South	42.3	51.2	7.2	14.4
West	9.9	15.9	1.8	4.3
Crowded (over one person per room)				
Northeast	12.1	12.8	4.5	5.6
North Central	6.7	11.2	4.1	9.8
South	10.7	18.4	6.5	8.3
West	8.8	21.4	5.8	7.1
At least one housing problem				
Northeast	58.1	90.9	38.2	63.7
North Central	60.1	88.3	42.3	61.7
South	69.3	90.8	45.5	54.9
West	49.4	87.0	39.7	41.9
Multiple housing problems				
Northeast	13.4	33.8	3.0	17.6
North Central	10.1	21.7	5.0	9.3
South	17.3	42.1	3.2	10.4
West	6.8	24.7	1.1	6.5

welfare only households paying more than 30 percent of their income for housing in this region is about 10 percent lower than the proportion observed in the Northeast and North Central states. and about equal to observed in the Northeast and North Central states, and about equal to the proportion observed in the West. However, the prevalence of substandard housing is dramatically higher in the South, with about half of all welfare only households living in physically inadequate housing. This rate is two to four times as high as the rates observed elsewhere in the country. Similarly, the prevalence of households with multiple housing needs is dramatically higher in the South. Although the prevalence of housing problems also varies for households enrolled in assisted housing programs, the variations are not as large as those observed under traditional income assistance programs.

Housing programs thus help to reduce the regional differences in the housing situations of program recipients. However, the regional patterns displayed by welfare households not enrolled in housing programs may reflect factors other than variations in payment standards. As is evident in table 3.9, households above the poverty line also have a higher incidence of substandard housing units in the South, as well as a higher incidence of multiple housing needs. Variations in the overall condition of the housing stock may thus explain part of the regional variations observed in the housing conditions of those on welfare.

VARIATIONS BY TENURE

Thus far we have treated the welfare only population as a homogeneous group. However, as shown in table 3.1 above, nearly 40 percent of all such households own their homes, and may face significantly different housing circumstances than those who rent. Table 3.10 presents information on both the income and housing situations of this subgroup of the population, stratified by the household's tenure. The figures in the chart reveal some striking differences between the two groups.

To begin with, renters in the welfare only population have substantially lower incomes than their counterparts who own their homes. About 47 percent of the renters report incomes of less than $5,000 per year, and only 10 percent report incomes of $15,000 or more. These income figures resemble those reported by households receiving both income and housing subsidies, and are considerably below the incomes of homeowners on welfare and of households that receive housing assistance alone. Thus, the targeting of multiple subsidies to the lowest income groups reflects the fact that housing programs are geared to renters. However, there are substantial numbers of equally needy renters on welfare who are not now benefiting from housing assistance because such subsidies are not entitlements, but are distributed on a first come, first served basis.

Table 3.9   HOUSING CONDITIONS OF THE NON-POOR POPULATION, 1983

Housing problem	Northeast	North Central	South	West
Affordability				
Paying over 30 percent	25.6	21.1	22.7	27.5
Paying over 50 percent	10.8	9.4	10.9	11.3
Substandard	6.3	3.7	10.0	3.7
Crowded	1.8	1.2	2.1	2.9
At least one housing problem	32.3	25.5	33.1	32.5
Multiple housing problems	2.0	0.9	2.4	1.8

Note: Includes households with income above the poverty line and excludes assisted households.

Despite their lower incomes, the housing costs of renters are about the same as the housing costs of those who own their homes. As a result, some 80 percent of renters receiving welfare but not housing assistance pay more than 30 percent of their income for rent, and 57 percent pay over half. The affordability problem within this group is thus widespread and severe. In contrast, about 47 percent of owners pay more than 30 percent, and 28 percent pay more than half. These ratios are close to those observed among households receiving both income and housing assistance, but considerably above those experienced by non-welfare households with housing assistance.

The incidence of crowding and substandard housing are relatively similar between owners and renters. About the same proportion of units have been classified as substandard, and the incidence of major and minor problems is about the same. A somewhat higher fraction of renters than owners have more than one person per room, but the differences are relatively small (15 versus 9 percent). Thus, the higher prevalence of multiple housing problems among households who rent than households who own (30 versus 13 percent) is because most (eight out of every ten) renters have a housing cost burden that exceeds 30 percent.

Table 3.10 SELECTED DEMOGRAPHIC AND HOUSING CHARACTERISTICS BY
TENURE: HOUSEHOLDS WITH INCOME ASSISTANCE BUT NO
HOUSING SUBSIDIES, 1983

Category	Renters	Owners
Household income		
Under $5,000	46.9	29.0
$5,000 to $9,999	33.1	28.5
$10,000 to $14,999	9.9	13.0
$15,000 to $19,999	4.6	8.1
$20,000 and over	5.4	21.5
	100.0	100.0
Monthly housing costs		
Under $100	3.7	19.9
$100 to $200	23.5	25.5
$201 to $300	34.4	20.2
$301 and over	38.4	34.5
	100.0	100.0
Mean costs (dollars)	280	275
Housing cost-to-income ratio		
Under 0.25	13.3	45.0
0.25 to 0.30	6.5	8.5
0.31 to 0.40	11.5	11.0
0.41 to 0.50	11.9	7.8
0.50 and over	56.7	27.8
	100.0	100.0
Mean ratio	0.585	0.400
Persons per room		
Under 1.0	84.5	90.5
1.1 to 1.5	11.4	7.4
1.6 to 2.0	3.1	1.6
2.1 and over	1.0	0.5
	100.0	100.0
Percent substandard	29.0	25.8
Fail major (i.e., structural problems)	8.6	8.8
Fail minor (i.e., maintenance problems)	25.0	23.1
Fail both	4.7	6.2

Table 3.10 (continued)

Category	Renters	Owners
Number of problems		
None	10.7	38.3
One		
Quality only	5.7	14.5
Affordability only	50.3	29.5
Crowding only	3.1	4.9
Two	26.1	11.9
Three	4.1	1.1
	100.0	100.0

VARIATIONS BY WELFARE PROGRAM

The housing situation of welfare recipients also differs according to the type of income assistance received (table 3.11). Although all three groups devote a disproportionate share of their incomes to housing, AFDC families generally pay the highest proportion of their income for housing, while SSI recipients pay the lowest. Two factors may explain the lower cost burdens of SSI households: the more generous shelter payments of SSI and the higher rate of homeownership among SSI households. Since elderly homeowners are likely to have paid off their mortgages, their housing costs mainly consist of utility costs. The incidence of crowding is also highest among AFDC households. Some 21 percent of all such families live in units with more than one person per room, compared to 12 percent for GA recipients and 5 percent for households with SSI.

Housing quality, in contrast, appears to be more of a problem for the SSI population. Some 36 percent of all such households live in housing classified as substandard, and 16 percent live in units with major structural defects. In contrast, about 25 percent of all AFDC and GA households live in physically inadequate units, and 6 to 8 percent live in units requiring major structural repairs. The higher incidence of substandard housing among SSI recipients in part reflects their greater tendency to live in the South. However, even within the South the incidence of substandard housing is significantly higher for SSI households than it is for those with General Assistance or AFDC.

Table 3.12 compares the actual housing expenditures of AFDC, SSI, and GA recipients to AFDC, SSI, and GA shelter allowances, as

Table 3.11 HOUSING CONDITIONS OF THE WELFARE POPULATION BY
PROGRAM

Category	Aid to Families with Dependent Children	Supplemental Security Income	General Assistance
Affordability			
Paying over 30 percent	83.0	53.0	70.0
Paying over 50 percent	61.0	28.0	51.0
Substandard	25.0	36.0	27.0
Fail major	6.0	16.0	8.0
Fail minor	23.0	31.0	23.0
Fail both	4.0	11.0	5.0
Crowded	21.0	5.0	12.0
At least one housing problem	91.0	71.0	79.0
Multiple housing problems	30.0	17.0	24.0
Memorandum items			
Percent owning home	23.0	53.0	31.0
Sample size	769	954	933

Note: Estimates exclude households in subsidized housing.

well as to the minimum FMRs for two bedroom units[11] and efficiency
apartments. Compared to other welfare households, SSI recipients
spend close to the shelter allowances that have been budgeted under that
program, but considerably less (i.e., 11 to 29 percent) than the
expenditure levels allowed under the applicable FMRs. AFDC families
spend considerably more than the shelter allowances budgeted under
AFDC, and up to 13 percent more than the applicable FMRs. But
despite the fact that AFDC recipients are devoting a relatively high
proportion of their incomes to housing, the quality of their units is not
dramatically better than the quality of units occupied by SSI recipients,
and a sizable fraction live in crowded conditions. Since the prototypical
AFDC recipient is a female household head with children, whereas SSI
and GA recipients are often single person households, this pattern may
well reflect a relative scarcity of standard units with two or more
bedrooms.

Table 3.12 COMPARISON OF ACTUAL EXPENDITURES AND FMRs,
WELFARE ONLY, 1983

Welfare households	Average housing costs[a]	Fair Market Rent	Shelter allowance
Receiving AFDC only, household of four			
Northeast	319	286	178
North Central	303	268	141
South	279	276	77
West	324	326	208
Receiving SSI only, living alone			
Northeast	186	208	144
North Central	159	180	117
South	127	180	109
West	180	236	157
Receiving GA only, living alone			
Northeast	204	208	149
North Central	202	180	111
South	122	180	76
West	201	236	145

a. These are "gross" costs, which include utilities for renters and non-mortgage payments for owners.

AFDC families clearly end up in last place with respect to the overall incidence of housing problems among the welfare population. Some 91 percent of all such households have at least one housing problem, and 30 percent have more than one. SSI recipients do somewhat better; 71 percent of all such households have at least one housing problem, and 17 percent have two or more. The incidence of housing problems among GA recipients lies between these two.

The relatively poorer performance of AFDC and GA households may reflect differences in the underlying payment standards. As described in chapter 2, shelter allowances under SSI are closer to the FMR than shelter allowances under AFDC or GA. But it may simply reflect fundamental differences in the supply of housing. Nationally, the percent of households with a housing problem is considerably higher for female-headed households (44 percent) than it is for the elderly (28 percent). Even if one excludes very low-income households, female-headed households have an incidence of housing problems that is almost twice as high as that of the elderly population (21 versus 11 percent).

RELATIONSHIP OF HOUSING OUTCOMES TO TYPE
OF ASSISTANCE AND HOUSEHOLD CHARACTERISTICS

To this point, we have described the characteristics of households receiving different types of shelter assistance and the housing outcomes associated with these different shelter assistance approaches. Yet, because of differences in the characteristics of recipients in assistance programs, it is difficult to judge whether these differential outcomes arise because of differences between types of assistance or because of other characteristics that distinguish recipients from each other. Thus, we have not fully addressed two questions. The first concerns the relative effects of housing versus welfare assistance on housing outcomes, after controlling for household characteristics; the second is whether the effectiveness of the type of assistance a household receives depends on that household's characteristics (e.g., age and composition).

To investigate these questions, we tested a number of parallel regression models on three different types of households: those where the head of the household is elderly, those in which children are present, and all other non-elderly households.[12] The three outcome variables in these models were crowding, affordability, and housing quality.[13] The explanatory variables included various demographic and economic attributes of the household and, of greatest interest, the type of assistance received: welfare only, housing only, or both.[14]

Guided by the descriptive data, we tested several alternative specifications of these models. For example, because assistance programs may be associated with different outcomes for owners and renters (particularly affordability for elderly recipients, as shown earlier in table 3.11), we tested each model twice: once including all households, and once only including renters. In addition, the large differences in .housing outcomes by region suggest that receiving welfare assistance in the South, for example, may not be equivalent to receiving such assistance in the Northeast--because of differences in either the generosity of payments, the overall characteristics of the housing stock, or some other factor. To account for such regional differences, we examined whether the effectiveness of each type of assistance depended on the region of residence.[15]

Households receiving housing assistance only and households receiving housing and welfare assistance had substantially better housing outcomes than households on welfare only, when other variables were controlled.[16] For example, receiving housing assistance is associated with between one-half and one fewer physical housing deficiency than if only welfare assistance were received, and a decline of 9 percent to 21 percent in the percentage of income devoted to housing costs. Differences in the effects of type of assistance on all elderly households compared to renters only are not statistically significant,[17] indicating that exclusion of elderly owners (with lower housing burdens) from the renter-only models does not introduce major bias. Thus, housing assistance appears to have consistently strong and positive effects on housing outcomes for various types of households, in contrast to welfare assistance.

We could find only two instances in which type of assistance had differential effects on the housing outcomes of different household groups.[18] The first is that receiving welfare assistance only is associated with greater increases in housing cost burdens for households with children compared to the elderly (on average, an increase of about 18 percent versus 10 percent, respectively). These differences were not significant when renters were tested separately, probably because elderly owners without mortgage debt receiving SSI were excluded. The second is that the opposite pattern emerges for housing quality. Receiving welfare only is associated with a greater increase in the number of physical deficiencies for elderly households than for households with children (roughly an increase of one housing deficiency for the elderly versus .5 of a housing deficiency for households with children). These effects apply to both renters and to all households. We could find no instances of differential effects between households with children and other non-elderly households, or between the elderly and other non-elderly households.

No clear pattern emerged when we took explicit account of the possible interaction between type of assistance and region, with one consistent exception. Receiving welfare assistance only in the South is associated with greater increases in housing cost burdens for households with children than for the elderly or other non-elderly households, but greater increases in housing deficiencies for the elderly than for households with children. To some extent, these regional differences may underlie the general results described above.

RELATIONSHIP OF HOUSING CONDITIONS TO SHELTER ALLOWANCES

The multiple regression results strongly support the findings that welfare programs alone are ineffective at achieving positive housing outcomes for recipients. However, because the generosity of the welfare shelter grant could not be taken into account in these models,[19] we have not yet addressed the question of whether income assistance can be as effective as housing assistance at achieving minimal housing standards for the poor. This question is fundamental to any consideration of restructuring shelter assistance policy.

To look more directly at the impact of shelter allowances per se, we examined the housing situation of the welfare only population in the 25 SMSAs that were included in the metropolitan files of the 1982 and 1983 Annual Housing Surveys.[20] As shown in table 3.13, the SMSAs vary in terms of size, geographic region, and overall incidence of housing needs. The shelter allowances available for welfare recipients in these markets also reflect a mix of relatively generous and stringent standards.

We began by examining the simple relationship between the size of the shelter allowance implicit or explicit in the welfare payment and the housing problems of those on welfare. Since these metropolitan data do not identify the specific source of assistance payments, the shelter allowances are weighted averages of the specific payment standards under AFDC, SSI, and GA, where the weights reflect the relative importance of the different programs within each site.[21]

There is no simple relationship between the housing conditions of welfare recipients and the overall generosity of the area's welfare system in relationship to the cost of standard housing. Figure 3.1 plots the overall proportion of welfare households with at least one housing problem against the ratio of the shelter allowance to the local FMR.[22] At one extreme, New York City has the highest overall incidence of housing problems despite its relatively generous payment standard. At the other extreme, households in Denver fare relatively well, despite the fact that payments are low. The same conclusion emerges if one considers specific types of housing problems. As shown in table 3.14, none of the different measures of housing need is significantly correlated with the generosity of the local shelter allowance.

Of course, other factors such as the cost and quality of the housing stock can be expected to exercise a strong influence on the housing situation of welfare recipients in any given market. While such influences are difficult to model--and, indeed, require a richer body of data than we had available for the current research--we controlled for them to some extent by estimating four simple regression equations in each of which the dependent variable was the proportion of the welfare population with a specific type of housing problem. The independent variables were: (1) the ratio of the shelter allowance to the local FMR and (2) the proportion of the unassisted non-poverty population with the same type of housing problem. The latter variable was included to approximate variations in the overall cost and quality of the housing stock.

The results of this analysis are summarized in table 3.15, where each column represents a different regression equation. The proportion of the welfare population in crowded or physically substandard housing

Table 3.13 CHARACTERISTICS OF SAMPLE SITES

Region	Number of households (thousands)	Percent receiving income assistance[a]	Percent shelter payment: FMR[b]	All households				Welfare households			
				Percent with housing problem	Percent paying more than 30%	Percent crowded	Percent sub-standard	Percent with housing problem	Percent paying more than 30%	Percent crowded	Percent substandard
Northeast											
Hartford	236	3.5	0.51	26.8	22.4	1.8	4.1	81.0	76.7	12.7	20.8
New York	3,910	7.1	0.60	46.5	33.9	5.2	14.8	89.2	80.4	15.4	43.8
Paterson	452	2.9	0.30	28.1	22.3	2.5	5.0	83.1	73.9	18.5	28.3
Philadelphia[c]	1,638	7.5	0.37	29.8	23.7	2.6	6.3	76.6	67.8	13.2	22.8
Rochester	310	5.4	0.63	23.1	18.9	1.7	4.3	73.3	66.1	9.1	26.1
North Central											
Chicago	2,437	6.8	0.30	33.3	27.4	4.1	5.0	84.2	77.5	15.7	21.7
Cincinnati[c]	500	5.6	0.32	26.0	20.8	2.9	4.1	78.7	69.6	16.8	17.2
Columbus	346	5.3	0.32	25.5	21.3	1.8	3.4	73.4	63.4	10.9	13.5
St. Louis[c]	819	4.6	0.49	24.1	19.5	2.8	3.6	84.9	67.5	26.3	17.7
Kansas City[c]	482	3.8	0.37	22.1	17.9	2.1	3.8	67.1	56.5	8.3	17.5
South											
Baltimore	760	5.2	0.29	26.3	21.2	1.9	5.1	70.7	57.7	13.4	23.1
Louisville	300	4.4	0.34	24.8	21.1	2.0	3.7	71.6	62.2	12.2	16.6
Miami	601	7.1	0.26	49.9	37.8	6.7	8.2	77.3	70.3	21.7	10.8
Atlanta	637	3.2	0.31	29.5	22.5	2.2	7.3	78.0	59.7	16.1	31.5
New Orleans	426	5.5	0.30	43.4	24.4	5.2	23.6	81.2	61.9	18.6	52.9
Houston	1,147	2.6	0.29	40.7	22.8	5.4	18.8	76.1	55.1	25.7	54.1

Table 3.13 (continued)

Region	Number of households (thousands)	Percent receiving income assistance[a]	Percent shelter payment: FMR[b]	All households				Welfare households			
				Percent with housing problem	Percent paying more than 30%	Percent crowded	Percent sub-standard	Percent with housing problem	Percent paying more than 30%	Percent crowded	Percent substandard
West											
Denver	639	2.6	0.31	29.2	25.7	1.5	2.4	64.9	57.4	9.2	1.8
Honolulu	238	5.1	0.47	40.7	31.7	8.2	3.8	88.2	75.1	29.7	14.0
Portland[c]	485	3.5	0.39	28.9	22.4	1.6	4.3	74.0	63.2	10.6	11.7
Sacramento	405	8.0	0.52	31.1	26.5	2.9	2.5	70.6	63.3	12.9	8.7
Seattle	639	3.8	0.54	25.8	20.6	1.6	2.9	66.3	59.6	10.6	4.5
San Antonio	344	4.2	0.29	44.4	21.7	6.3	24.9	86.3	48.6	19.2	67.9
San Bernardino	570	8.7	0.45	30.7	25.0	4.7	3.3	68.0	56.0	15.3	8.3
San Diego	685	7.0	0.40	35.5	30.4	3.6	3.2	73.9	63.0	12.3	11.3
San Francisco	1,285	5.2	0.42	33.6	27.8	3.5	5.1	72.1	61.6	13.9	17.1

Source: The 1982 and 1983 SMSA American Housing Surveys.

a. Excluding those with housing assistance.
b. Weighted average of the shelter payment to FMR ratio for AFDC, SSI, and GA.
c. Although these six SMSAs cross state boundaries, the large majority of the population in each resides in a single state. Therefore, estimates of welfare program shelter payments and HUD FMRs pertain to this state. (It is worth noting that in five of the six SMSAs, more than 75 percent of the SMSA's population is located in one state. But even in the one exception, Kansas City, where the proportion falls to 67 percent, the FMRs for the two relevant states (Missouri and Kansas) are identical as are the SSI shelter payments.)

Figure 3.1 GENEROSITY OF SHELTER PAYMENT VERSUS PROPORTION OF
HOUSEHOLDS WITH NEED

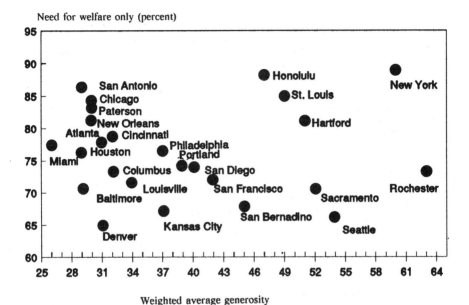

Need for welfare only (percent)

Weighted average generosity

Note: Excludes households receiving housing assistance.

Table 3.14 CORRELATION BETWEEN MEASURES OF NEED AND THE
GENEROSITY OF THE SHELTER ALLOWANCE (percent)

	Correlation coefficient	Significance level
Welfare households with a housing problem	0.022	n.s.
Welfare households paying more than 30 percent	0.314	n.s.
Welfare households that are crowded	-0.160	n.s.
Welfare households in substandard housing	-0.207	n.s.

Source: The 1982 and 1983 SMSA American Housing Surveys.

Note: Shelter allowance is expressed as fractions of the local FMRs. The sample is households receiving income but not housing assistance.

n.s. = Not significant at the 0.05 level.

Table 3.15 REGRESSIONS RELATING THE HOUSING CONDITIONS OF THE
WELFARE POPULATION TO THE GENEROSITY OF THE .
SHELTER PAYMENT

Independent variables	Dependent variables			
	Percent of welfare population paying more than 30 percent	Percent of welfare population crowded	Percent of welfare population in sub-standard units	Percent of welfare population with a hous-ing problem
Housing conditions of the population with incomes above the poverty line				
Percent paying more than 30 percent	0.435 (0.314)	--	--	--
Percent crowded	--	3.048** (0.597)	--	--
Percent in substandard housing	--	--	2.887** (0.296)	--
Total percent with a housing need	--	--	--	0.391* (0.174)
Ratio of Shelter Allowance to FMR	0.225 (0.144)	-0.055 (0.075)	0.094 (0.144)	0.061 (0.127)
Constant	48.48** (7.70)	11.32** (3.37)	3.827 (6.48)	64.7** (7.12)
$\bar{R}^2$	.17	.55	.82	.19

Source: The 1982 and 1983 SMSA American Housing Surveys.

Note: Excludes households receiving housing assistance.

** Significant at 0.05
* Significant at 0.10

was significantly related to the proportion of the non-poverty population
experiencing that problem (see columns 2 and 3); however, variations
in the size of the shelter allowance did not appear to affect the overall
incidence of such problems. Neither variable was significant in the

"affordability" equation (column 1), which may stem from the fact that even in the most generous site considered, the size of the budgeted shelter allowance was only about 60 percent of the cost of standard housing.

The housing problems of the welfare population undoubtedly reflect their limited resources. Nevertheless, our analysis suggests that simply increasing the size of the shelter allowances under AFDC, SSI, and GA will not automatically foster housing goals. While our tests are admittedly crude, our findings are consistent with the results of more elaborate analyses conducted under the auspices of the Experimental Housing Allowance Program (10; 11). Such studies found that poor households faced with a moderate increase in their disposable income will not typically choose to upgrade their housing units. Since the poor are already devoting a disproportionate share of their incomes to housing, they tend to use their additional income to reduce this effective burden, as opposed to moving to better, but presumably more expensive living arrangements.

Thus, at least within the range of payment levels represented by our sample, although higher allowances will obviously help to address the issue of affordability, which affects the largest proportion of the poor, they may have little effect on the incidence of crowding and substandard dwellings among households on welfare. If one wishes to improve the *housing* situation of the nation's poor, simply increasing the shelter allowance may not be the answer.

Notes

1. The analysis in this chapter is based on calendar, not fiscal, years.
2. While this fraction varies somewhat by type of income assistance received, the differences are fairly small--26 percent for AFDC, 24 percent for SSI, and 19 percent for General Assistance. The overlap between housing and income assistance is somewhat higher among renters. About 32 percent of all renters on welfare live in publicly subsidized housing.

3. There has always been a particular interest in the residential mobility of welfare households. A sizable body of research, for example, is devoted to the role of inter-state differences in welfare generosity in the mobility decisions of welfare eligibles. A broader set of policy questions includes whether there are large disparities in the mobility rates of the poor (both assisted and unassisted) and the non-poor, the circumstances that prompt poor households to move, and the outcomes of these moves; that is, whether movers are better or worse off as a result.
4. In addition to eviction due to tenant problems, this category includes moves caused by increases in rents, condominium conversion and building rehabilitation.
5. Defined as more than one person per room.
6. The comparison of monthly gross rents is limited to renters because the AHS does not contain monthly housing cost data on the previous residence if it was owned.
7. Another possible source of high housing cost burdens is the income certification process. One example, noted in chapter 2, is counting shelter payment maximums as income even

when the actual payment to the recipient is less than the maximum. More generally, the welfare rent provision leads to ratios that exceed 30 percent for recipients in as paid states.

8. As with the FMR, we have relied on an established measure of housing quality for the analysis. Although the measure has several components, it is applied here as a dichotomous "pass/fail" test because that is the way the standard is applied by HUD to ascertain if units are eligible for housing subsidies.

The elements of this housing quality standard are as follows:
- a) Unit lacks or shares complete plumbing facilities.
- b) Unit lacks adequate provision for sewage disposal. The unit must be connected with a public sewer, septic tank, cesspool, or chemical toilet.
- c) Unit lacks or shares complete kitchen facilities.
- d) Has two or more structural problems:
  Leaking roof.
  Leaking basement.
  Open cracks or holes in interior walls or ceiling.
  Holes in the interior floors.
  Peeling paint or broken plaster over one square foot on an interior wall.
  Evidence of mice or rats in last 90 days.
- e) Has two or more common area problems:
  No working light fixtures in common hallway.
  Loose, broken, or missing stairs.
  Broken or missing stair railings.
  No elevator in building (for units two or more floors from main building entrance in building four or more stories high).
- f) Unit is heated mainly by unvented room heaters which burn gas, oil, or kerosene.
- g) Unit has had three or more toilet breakdowns of six hours or more in the past 90 days.
- h) Unit had three or more heating breakdowns lasting six hours or more last winter.
- i) Lacks electricity.
- j) One or more rooms without a working wall outlet.
- k) Fuses blown or circuit breakers tripped three or more times during last 90 days.
- l) Exposed wiring in house.

9. See appendix F for a discussion of alternative quality measures.

10. Although the AHS data do not enable one to distinguish between different program types, the relatively small proportion of households living in units with multiple maintenance deficiencies could well be in the older public housing stock. Theoretically, the survey could be used for this purpose. However, households apparently have difficulty distinguishing between public housing per se and other types of housing assistance (e.g., Section 8).

11. To facilitate comparisons with shelter allowances and FMRs (which are geared to family size and bedroom count), we have restricted the data on GA and SSI to single-person households and on AFDC to four-person households. Note that the national AHS data tape does not identify the state in which households reside. As a result, the average FMRs and shelter allowances appearing in the chart are regional averages derived from the survey data presented in chapter 2.

12. As is true throughout our analysis, only households receiving welfare or housing assistance were included.

13. Each of these housing outcomes was recoded into continuous form so that ordinary least squares regression could be used. Recoding crowding and affordability was straightforward; recoding the housing quality standard required weighting each of the minor maintenance deficiencies by a factor of .5 since housing units must fail two of these elements to be considered substandard. (See appendix E for the definition of housing quality used.)

14. Specifically, the independent variables were: race (whether white; whether black); metropolitan status (whether central city; whether in rest of SMSA); household size; and

income. Regressions on all households (both owners and renters) included a housing tenure variable (whether own). Models applied to households with children were tested twice: once controlling for the sex of the household head (whether female), and once not. Results were very similar. Finally, the crowding models were restricted to households that included at least two persons.

15. Statistically, we tested the interaction between type of assistance and region. Since there are three types of assistance (welfare only, housing only, and both) and four regions, we specified these interaction terms as a pattern variable of eleven dummy variables (e.g., whether welfare, Northeast; whether welfare, North Central; etc.). The omitted category was whether welfare, South.

16. See the regression coefficients shown in appendix F for one specification. Other specifications had similar results.

17. We relied on a crude test of differences in effects of assistance programs on affordability between all elderly households and elderly renters. We determined whether the coefficient on the type of assistance variable for all elderly households fell within plus or minus two standard errors of the comparable coefficient for elderly renters. Differences between coefficients that fell within this interval were judged to be insignificant at the .05 level.

18. That is, these coefficients for the different household types were within plus or minus two standard errors of each other, using the same approach described in the previous footnote.

19. As noted earlier, state of residence is not available on the 1983 national AHS files used in these analyses.

20. The second phase of the project will extend the analysis to the full 59 SMSAs that are surveyed as part of the metropolitan area data collections of the AHS. The present analysis was restricted to 25 SMSAs mainly because of data limitations. The SMSA surveys are conducted in three-year cycles. We included the SMSAs in the most recently released cycles.

21. The weights were derived by examining the composition of household types within the welfare only population. In particular, we estimated the relative importance of AFDC, SSI, and GA within a given site by examining the relative number of: (1) female-headed households with children; (2) households with an elderly head; and (3) non-elderly, single males.

22. This "combined" ratio is a weighted average of the following ratios: (1) the ratio of the AFDC shelter allowance for a family of four to the two-bedroom FMR; (2) the ratio of the SSI shelter allowance for an individual living alone to the zero bedroom FMR; and (3) the ratio of the GA shelter allowance for an individual living alone to the zero bedroom FMR.

4

DIRECTIONS FOR FUTURE POLICY

If the nation's shelter assistance system is to be effectively reformed, any policy must take explicit note of the two streams of government financing for low-income housing: the housing stream and the welfare stream. As we noted at the outset, the welfare system--through the explicit and implicit shelter allowances that welfare recipients receive as part of their public assistance benefits--spends at least $10 billion a year in housing assistance, roughly the same as HUD.

This two-pronged system as it currently operates has several serious inadequacies. First, although both the housing and welfare systems take similar approaches to shelter assistance, namely, cash assistance to needy households, they do not coordinate their activities. This leads to a substantial overlap of 1.3 million households (in 1983) who received two shelter benefits--one through their welfare payments and the other through their housing certificates or vouchers.

The existence of double benefits for a portion of the eligible population is not the only aspect of the system that is unfair. Inequities arise also because of the structure of each component of the system. Under welfare programs, geography rather than need plays the major role in determining the amount of shelter assistance a beneficiary receives. But while some jurisdictions are more generous than others, almost none provides shelter payments that equal the cost of standard quality housing as measured by HUD's Fair Market Rents (FMR). AFDC shelter payments average only 50 percent of the applicable FMR; SSI and GA hover around 66 percent. Under HUD programs, recipients do gain access to standard housing regardless of geography; but only a small fraction of those in need receive benefits. Thus, in 1983, there were 2.8 million renters on welfare who did not receive housing assistance but who had incomes that were just as low as those who did.

A third problem with the current system concerns the housing outcomes for recipients. As a first approximation, it is fair to say that housing assistance recipients gain access to decent and affordable dwellings. In contrast, welfare households often spend more than half of their incomes on housing and many live in substandard units. Furthermore, welfare recipients living in metropolitan areas with generous shelter allowances often fare no better than average. This pattern is consistent with the findings of the income maintenance and housing allowance experiments of the 1970s, which showed that unrestricted cash grants had only a minimal effect on improving housing conditions.

DIRECTIONS FOR A RESTRUCTURED SHELTER SUBSIDY

What should a restructured shelter assistance policy look like? The second phase of the project will answer this question in detail. But we already can identify some general directions for a restructured approach. First, the new structure must be more equitable than the one it replaces. Neither the welfare system nor the housing system ranks high on equity grounds. Under welfare, there is enormous variation in the housing subsidies received by households both within and between programs. As a general rule, under housing programs, households are assisted on a first come-first served basis.[1] Although housing subsidies are targeted to low-income households, in 1983 there were 2.8 million renters on welfare who did not receive housing program assistance but who had incomes that were just as low as those participating in housing programs. At the other end of the range, as noted, roughly 1.3 million households received both welfare and housing subsidies.

One way the inequities in the current system could be addressed is by reducing or eliminating the regional disparities in welfare payments. This general theme has been echoed in recent proposals addressing the disparities in AFDC benefits.

The appropriate benefit level of such a new, standardized welfare system is obviously subject to debate, but our data indicate that shelter allowances under the major welfare programs would have to be raised by between 50 and 100 percent, depending on the state, to meet the standards employed by HUD. Our data also suggest that this increase would cost about $10 billion a year.[2] While these estimates are extremely crude, if HUD continued to serve a significant number of recipients who were not on welfare, this modification would appear to require an increase in total expenditures on housing assistance (including indirect subsidies available through welfare) of roughly 50 percent.

A more equitable distribution of housing benefits can be achieved in various ways. One option would be to develop a two-tiered payment system. Under such a system, a minimal shelter allowance could be available to all recipients, but only households in units which met program standards would receive the full subsidy amount. For example, the lower payment would be available to households who, for a variety of personal and unpredictable reasons, simply cannot find, or do not choose to live in, a housing unit that meets program standards. If the lower payment standard were about the same as the current national average (about 60 percent of the FMR), the program's shelter costs would probably drop to about $7 billion per year.[3]

But reducing the regional disparities in welfare payments is not sufficient to insure the equity of shelter assistance policy. Two inequities would still remain: double subsidies for some, and HUD subsidies for only a subset of the eligible population. Resolving these problems will undoubtedly require much closer coordination between housing and welfare policy, funding and personnel than has existed in the past. Such coordination could also improve the efficiency and effectiveness of shelter assistance policy, as well as its equity.

ENDNOTE

The foregoing discussion assumes that housing goals remain a part of the nation's public policy agenda. Judging by the events of the last several years, this is not at all clear. There has not been a federal housing act for several years, virtually all HUD construction subsidy programs have been terminated, funding for existing demand-side programs is meager, and the 1986 tax reform legislation makes the future of private sector involvement in the provision of low-income housing uncertain at best.

We believe a case can be made for restructuring housing policy. This case rests on several factors: the inequities and inefficiencies of the current two-pronged system, the ineffectiveness of welfare programs at achieving housing goals, the realization that transfer payments earmarked for housing are substantially different from untied income transfers, and most fundamentally, the motivations that underlie society's support for programs that assist the poor. We believe the case is compelling.

Notes

1.   In general, eligibility for public housing and Section 8 rent assistance is determined by household income. Households that meet income eligibility criteria are placed on a public housing or Section 8 waiting list. Other conditions of the eligible households are ascertained before priorities are determined. Local housing authorities determine "preferences" based on applicants' current housing conditions. These preferences include the following: without housing; about to be without housing; and in substandard housing. Local housing authorities may take other conditions into consideration before assigning priority, so long as the conditions are consistent with the objectives of Title IV of the Civil Rights Act of 1964.

2.   In 1983, 78 percent of the welfare population, or about 4.6 million households, did not participate in housing programs. A housing voucher currently costs about $3,800 per year, which means that the gross cost of serving this group would be roughly $17.4 billion a year. However, since the welfare system already spends about $10 billion a year on shelter allowances, the net cost would be lower. If 78 percent of these indirect subsidies are going to the welfare only population, the costs of raising their shelter allowances to the levels employed by HUD would drop to about $9.6 billion per year (i.e., $17.4 billion for the new vouchers less $7.8 billion of existing assistance).

3.   This estimate assumes that participation rates would be similar to those observed in the housing allowance experiment, which were 70 percent for renters and 76 percent for owners. Since 61 percent of the "welfare only" population are renters, this implies an average participation rate of 72 percent, which would reduce the estimated costs of a voucher-like program to about $6.9 billion (72 percent of the total costs with 100 percent participation). This estimate is similar to the $7.4 billion estimate derived by Katsura and Struyk (12) using a different methodology and a different data set.

APPENDICES

Appendix A   SUMMARY STATISTICS FOR FOUR PERSONS ON SHELTER ASSISTANCE UNDER AFDC, BY STATE, 1984-85 DATA (dollars unless otherwise noted)

	Standard of need	Payment level	Payment level / Standard of need	Shelter need	Shelter payment	Difference in shelter as compared to three persons (percent)	Shelter need / Standard of need	Shelter payment / Shelter need	HUD Fair Market Rents High	HUD Fair Market Rents Low	Shelter for four persons Low FMR for state
Alabama	480	147	.31	(144)	(44)	(.26)	(.30)	(.31)	356	254	(.17)
Alaska	800	800	1.00	(240)	(240)	.11	(.30)	(1.00)	693	588	(.41)
Arizona	282	282	1.00	112	112	(.20)	.40	1.00	445	328	.34
Arkansas	273	164	.60	40	24	0	.15	.60	331	228	.11
California	660	660	1.00	222	222	.05	.34	1.00	577	335	.66
Colorado	765	420	.55	207	113	.11	.27	.55	552	307	.37
Connecticut											
Region A (high)	636	636	1.00	265	265	.12	.42	1.00	491	363	.73
Region C (low)	534	534	1.00	162	162	.07	.30	1.00			.45
Delaware	336	336	1.00	101	101	.17	.30	1.00	421	361	.28
District of Columbia	798	399	.50	(239)	(120)	.22	(.30)	(.50)	440	440	.27
Florida	468	284	.61	135	82	.01	.29	.61	515	283	.29
Georgia	432	264	.61	(130)	(79)	(.17)	(.30)	(.61)	397	261	(.30)
Hawaii	546	546	1.00	265	265	.10	.49	1.00	552	507	.52
Idaho	627	344	.55	142	78	0	.23	.55	361	307	.25
Illinois	752	386	.51	297	155	-.02	.40	.52	572	247	.63
Indiana	375	316	.84	100	84	.04	.27	.84	367	292	.29
Iowa	578	419	.73	100	72	.08	.17	.72	382	287	.25
Kansas											
Group I (low)	363	363	1.00	76	76	0	.21	1.00	376	232	.33
Group II (high)	422	422	1.00	135	135	0	.32	1.00			.58
Kentucky	246	246	1.00	(74)	(74)	(.25)	(.30)	(1.00)	386	236	(.31)
Louisiana											
Region I (low)	658	217	.33	(197)	(65)	(.24)	(.30)	(.33)			(.29)
Region II (high)	712	234	.33	(214)	(70)	(.23)	(.30)	(.33)	375	228	(.31)

Appendix A (continued)

	Standard of need	Payment level	Payment level / Standard of need	Shelter need	Shelter payment	Difference in shelter as compared to three persons (percent)	Shelter need / Standard of need	Shelter payment / Shelter need	HUD Fair Market Rents High	HUD Fair Market Rents Low	Shelter for four persons Low FMR for state
Maine	640	465	.73	214	155	.26	.33	.72	450	339	.46
Maryland	520	376	.72	191	138	.20	.37	.72	572	418	.33
Massachusetts	490	463	.95	125	119	0	.26	.95	533	364	.33
Michigan									448	298	
Zone I (low)	564	516	.92	140	140	.22	.25	1.00	451	280	.47
Zone II (high)	628	575	.92	195	195	.15	.31	1.00	387	279	.65
Minnesota	611	611	1.00	(183)	(183)	(.17)	(.30)	(1.00)	385	232	(.65)
Mississippi	327	120	.37	60	22	.10	.18	.37	425	316	.08
Missouri	365	310	.85	(110)	(93)	(.16)	(.30)	(.85)	373	273	(.40)
Montana	513	425	.83	250	207	.26	.49	.83	528	423	.66
Nebraska	420	420	1.00	105	105	.02	.25	1.00			.38
Nevada	341	280	.82	(102)	(84)	(.20)	(.30)	(.82)			(.20)
New Hampshire									496	359	.39
Reg. Housing	442	442	1.00	141	141	0	.32	1.00			
Sub. Housing	418	418	1.00	174	174	0	.42	1.00			.48
New Jersey	443	443	1.00	(133)	(133)	(.17)	(.30)	(1.00)	548	370	(.36)
New Mexico	313	313	1.00	105	105	.19	.34	1.00	341	280	.38
New York									539	282	
New York City	528	528	1.00	270	270	.11	.51	1.00	(436)		.96
Erie County	457	457	1.00	199	199	.03	.44	1.00	(391)		.71
North Carolina	488	244	.50	(146)	(73)	(.09)	(.30)	(.50)	377	246	(.30)
North Dakota	454	454	1.00	114	114	0	.25	1.00	491	310	.37
Ohio	757	343	.45	(227)	(103)	(.24)	(.30)	(.45)	373	246	(.42)
Oklahoma									424	244	
A (high)	349	349	1.00	(105)	(105)	(.24)	(.30)	(1.00)			(.43)
B (low)	301	301	1.00	(90)	(90)	(.29)	(.36)	(1.00)			(.37)

Appendix A (continued)

	Standard of need	Payment level	Payment level / Standard of need	Shelter need	Shelter payment	Difference in shelter as compared to three persons (percent)	Shelter need / Standard of need	Shelter payment / Shelter need	HUD Fair Market Rents High	HUD Fair Market Rents Low	Shelter for four persons / Low FMR for state
Oregon	392	392	1.00	140	140	.21	.36	1.00	408	302	.46
Pennsylvania	724	429	.59	(217)	(129)	(.24)	(.30)	(.59)	402	237	(.54)
Rhode Island	484	484	1.00	(145)	(145)	(.14)	(.30)	(1.00)	420	361	(.40)
South Carolina	229	229	1.00	44	44	0	.19	1.00	377	279	.16
South Dakota	371	371	1.00	163	163	0	.44	1.00	364	285	.57
Tennessee	300	168	.56	74	51	.21	.30	.89	391	253	.20
Texas	593	201	.34	188	64	.14	.32	.34	434	244	.26
Utah	809	428	.53	297	157	.08	.37	.53	413	277	.57
Vermont	798	523	.66	263	173	0	.33	.66	478	351	.49
Virginia											
Group I (low)	331	298	.90	141	127	.13	.43	.90			.48
Group III (high)	422	379	.90	210	189	.09	.50	.90	415	266	.71
Washington	904	561	.62	471	292	.12	.52	.62	461	302	.97
West Virginia											
Plan II (high)	332	249	.75	63	47	.09	.19	.75	451	387	.12
Plan I (low)	236	170	.72	0	0	0	0				0
Wisconsin											
Area I (high)	749	637	.85	225	191	.19	(.30)	(.85)	451	273	.70
Area II (low)	723	618	.86	217	185	.19	(.30)	(.85)			.68
Wyoming	390	390	1.00	80	80	0	.21	1.00	478	307	.26

Source: Telephone interviews with state AFDC officials and state documents.

Notes:
1. State officials were interviewed in late 1984 and early 1985. The data reflect the standard of need and payment levels in effect at the time of the interview.
2. All AFDC payment levels are maximum allowable amounts.
3. Numbers in parentheses are estimates for states whose shelter needs and payment levels could not be extracted from state documents.
4. Need and payment standard shown is for Chicago; rest of Illinois uses a different need and payment standard.
5. HUD FMR data are for 2-bedroom units.
6. AFDC to FMR ratios (last column) are misleading in states with intra-state variations in AFDC payments: "High" versus "low" AFDC locations do not correspond to "high" and "low" FMR locations.

89

Appendix B FEDERAL SHARE OF AFDC, BY STATE, 1984-85

State	1984-85	State	1984-85
Alabama	72.14	Montana	64.41
Alaska	50.00	Nebraska	57.13
Arizona	61.21	Nevada	50.00
Arkansas	73.65	New Hampshire	59.45
California	50.00	New Jersey	50.00
Colorado	50.00	New Mexico	69.39
Connecticut	50.00	New York	50.00
Delaware	50.00	North Carolina	69.54
District		North Dakota	61.32
of Columbia	50.00	Ohio	55.44
Florida	58.14	Oklahoma	58.47
Georgia	67.43	Oregon	57.12
Hawaii	50.00	Pennsylvania	56.04
Idaho	67.28	Puerto Rico	75.00
Illinois	50.00	Rhode Island	58.17
Indiana	59.93	South Carolina	73.51
Iowa	55.24	South Dakota	68.31
Kansas	50.67	Tennessee	70.66
Kentucky	70.72	Texas	54.37
Louisiana	64.65	Utah	70.84
Maine	70.63	Vermont	59.37
Maryland	50.00	Virginia	56.53
Massachusetts	50.13	Washington	50.00
Michigan	50.70	West Virginia	70.57
Minnesota	52.67	Wisconsin	56.87
Mississippi	77.63	Wyoming	50.00
Missouri	61.40		

Source: Background Material and Data on Programs Within the Jurisdiction of the House Committee on Ways and Means (February 1985), pp. 356-57.

Appendix C   HOUSEHOLD CHARACTERISTICS OF ELIGIBLE
RECIPIENTS OF AFDC, BY STATE, 1984

Household Characteristics	Eligible States[a]
Eligible Children	All states
One needy parent or caretaker of child	All states except Mississippi
Second parent if one parent is incapacitated or principal earner is unemployed	All states except Alaska Mississippi, and West Virginia
Unemployed principal earner who is the parent of at least one child[b]	California, Colorado, Connecticut, Delaware, District of Columbia, Hawaii, Illinois, Iowa, Kansas, Maryland, Massachusetts, Michigan, Minnesota, Missouri, Nebraska, New Jersey, New York, Ohio, Pennsylvania, Rhode Island, Vermont, Washington, West Virginia, and Wisconsin
"Essential" persons[c]	Arkansas, California, District of Columbia, Hawaii, Illinois, Iowa, Kansas, Louisiana, Maryland, Massachusetts, Minnesota, Missouri, New Jersey, New York, North Carolina, Oregon, Pennsylvania, Puerto Rico, Utah, Vermont, Virginia, Washington, and Wisconsin

Source: U.S. Department of Health and Human Services. 1984. Research Tables from the Characteristics of State Plans for AFDC. Washington, D.C.

a.   All forty-eight states plus the District of Columbia, Alaska, Hawaii, and Puerto Rico.
b.   For states with AFDC-UP (unemployed persons).
c.   Any needy person living as a member of the family and performing an essential service. These persons are defined in various ways within the twenty-three states that include them in the grant.

ASSUMPTIONS AND DATA LIMITATIONS UNDERLYING
TABLE 2.4

1. The following states were deleted from the tabulations because they did not have a General Assistance program in fiscal 1984:   Alaska, Arkansas, Colorado, Idaho, Mississippi, North Carolina, Oklahoma, Tennessee, Vermont, and West Virginia.   It should be noted, however, that the majority of these states did offer some form of short-term Emergency Assistance.

2. Incomplete or no response was received from Alabama, Indiana, and South Carolina. These states, therefore, do not appear in the tabulations.

3. For the twenty states with statewide GA programs, the figures in table 2.4 are intended to reflect statewide estimates.

4. New Hampshire has been deleted from table 2.4 because of insufficient information.

5. Persons assumed to equal recipients.

6. The following assumptions were used to assign data to missing cells, by state:

State	Assumptions
New Jersey	Actual shelter percents and dollars based on the national averages of actual shelter percents for all states with complete data on each of these items, weighted by number of recipients per state.
New York	Number of cases based on national ratio of recipients to cases among those states with complete data on each of these items.
Rhode Island	Actual shelter percents and dollars based on national averages for all states with complete data on each of these items, weighted by number of recipients per state.
Iowa	Actual shelter dollars and percent represent Polk County.
Nebraska	Number of recipients based on national ratio of cases to recipients among those states with complete data on each of these items.
North Dakota	Actual GA and shelter payments represent Burleigh County.
South Dakota	Aggregate shelter percent assigned to actual shelter percent.
Wisconsin	Actual GA and shelter dollars represent Milwaukee.
Florida	Actual GA and shelter dollars represent Miami.
Georgia	Based on Fulton County.

State	Assumptions
Kentucky	Number of recipients based on national ratio of cases to recipients among those states with complete data on each of these items.
Louisiana	a. Actual shelter percents based on the national averages for all states with complete data on each of these items, weighted by number of recipients per state.
	b. All other entries in table based on telephone interview (no state documentation available).
Maryland	a. Actual shelter dollars derived from telephone interviews.
	b. Estimates represent the combination of two GA programs in the state: one for "unemployables" and the other for "employables."
Missouri	a. Actual shelter percent assumed to equal aggregate shelter percent.
	b. Number of recipients based on state official's view that only about 100 cases included two persons.
Texas	a. Number of recipients derived from telephone interviews.
	b. Actual GA and shelter dollars based on Harris County (Houston).
Montana	a. State documents show average number of cases equals average number of recipients.
	b. Actual shelter dollars represent an average for counties in the state, as reported in telephone interviews.
Nevada	a. Number of recipients based on assumption that Washoe recipients represent 20 percent of the state's GA recipients. This number was then blown up to an estimate of the total number of recipients in the state.
	b. Actual GA and shelter dollars represent Clark County.
Oregon	Number of recipients based on national ratio of cases to recipients among those states with complete data on each, of these items.

7. Data assignments were not made in cases where states were missing pairs of variables such as cases and recipients, or actual total and shelter GA payments.

8.   Regional and national GA-shelter dollars include some states where this value was assigned based on various assumptions. See listing under note 6 for details.

9.   Regional and national percents of GA actual dollars for shelter are weighted by the number of recipients in each state.

10.   Regional estimates of actual GA and GA-shelter payments are weighted by the number of recipients in each state.

11.   Shelter amounts include rent and utilities.

Appendix E   HOUSING QUALITY MEASUREMENT AND THE INCIDENCE OF
SUBSTANDARDNESS AMONG ASSISTED HOUSEHOLDS

Throughout this report, we have used one index of housing quality to measure the incidence of substandard housing conditions among assisted households. The specific index ranks high on external validity. It is based on the index developed by HUD's Office or Policy Development and Research in the early 1980s and incorporates several modest revisions that align it more closely to Section 8 existing housing standards.[1] The use of one index rather than several also makes sense on practical grounds since it simplifies both analysis and presentation.

Nevertheless, it is important to note that the concepts of "housing quality" or "housing adequacy" are not based on completely explicit criteria and have no precise, quantifiable definitions of where "bad" ends and "good" begins.[2] As a result, a large number of housing quality indices have been developed. Although there is a good deal of overlap among the core items in most of these indices (e.g., the presence or complete plumbing and kitchen facilities), there is also enough variation between them to suggest potential discrepancies in classifying dwellings as substandard.

To determine the extent to which such discrepancies arise, we re-estimated the incidence rates of substandard dwellings for nine additional housing quality indices cited in the literature or used in housing assistance programs. (Index definitions are provided in an attachment to this appendix.)

Table E.1 shows the rates of substandardness for each of these indices when applied to our five-category assistance variable. The index name "welfare and housing" is the one used throughout this paper and, therefore, sets the frame of reference for the other indices. Six of the indices produce estimates that are roughly comparable. These include: welfare and housing, elderly housing 1, elderly housing 2, HUD extended, HUD restricted, and CBO. The remaining four indices, however, diverge sharply. The Fair Market Rent and OMB indices consistently yield the highest rates of substandardness, while the HUD/Simonson index yields the lowest rates. Thus, depending on the housing quality index adopted, the fraction of "welfare only" households judged to reside in a deficient units ranges from a low of 18.8 percent (HUD/Simonson) to a high of 63.2 percent (FMR)--a gap of 44.4 percentage points. Furthermore, the discrepancy between the fraction of "welfare only" households in deficient units compared to "housing only" households varies between roughly 15 percentage points (HUD/Simonson) and 32 percentage points (New York state). In all cases, however, the incidence of substandardness is much higher among the welfare only group, ranging from about two to five times as great as that for households receiving housing assistance alone.

Table E.2 concentrates on rates of substandardness among the different subgroups of this "welfare only" population. Differences between indices persist when we restrict the sample to demographically more homogeneous groups. Most of the indices, however, produce little variation in rates of dwelling inadequacies between AFDC, SSI, AND GA-occupied units. A few, such as HUD extended, New York State and OMB, however, yield relatively large discrepancies.

---

1. In particular, it sets somewhat stricter tests for units to be judged as adequate compared to the HUD/Simonson index (e.g., HUD/Simonson req common area problems for a unit to be judged substandard while the revised index requires two or more such problems).
2. Newman, S. 1984. "Housing Research: Conceptual and Measurement Issues." In Survey Subjective Phenomena, edited by C. Turner and E. Martin. Vol. 2. New York: Russell Sage Foundation.

Table E.1 PERCENT OF UNITS RATED SUBSTANDARD, BY TYPE OF
ASSISTANCE (1983 National American Housing Survey)

	Total receiving income assistance	Total receiving housing assistance	Type of assistance		
			Income assistance only	Housing assistance only	Income & housing assistance
HUD/Simonson	16.4	5.3	18.8	3.4	8.2
HUD restricted	21.9	9.4	24.7	7.9	11.9
Elderly housing 1	22.8	9.3	25.6	7.3	12.6
CBO criteria	25.0	10.9	27.9	8.7	14.5
Welfare and housing	24.8	8.0	28.5	5.8	11.7
Elderly housing 2	29.1	9.3	34.1	7.8	11.7
HUD extended	29.3	9.2	34.1	7.2	12.5
New York state study	38.1	14.8	43.4	11.9	19.4
OMB criteria	54.9	35.9	58.2	31.5	43.1
Fair Market Rent	59.2	38.6	63.2	34.5	45.3

Table E.2 PERCENT OF UNITS RATED SUBSTANDARD ON ALTERNATIVE
HOUSING QUALITY INDICES AMONG "WELFARE ONLY"
HOUSEHOLDS, BY TYPE OF WELFARE (1983 National
American Housing Survey)

	AFDC only	SSI only	GA only	Other
HUD/Simonson	17.1	21.7	18.5	17.0
HUD restricted	24.5	28.9	22.6	21.9
Elderly housing 1	25.7	27.3	26.0	22.2
CBO criteria	28.6	28.7	29.0	23.6
Welfare and housing	25.0	36.0	26.8	24.2
Elderly housing 2	31.2	40.7	33.4	29.0
HUD extended	29.6	43.0	32.8	28.6
New York state study	38.8	54.1	42.1	35.5
OMB criteria	57.4	64.1	56.8	52.4
Fair Market Rent	63.2	68.2	62.2	56.7

HUD/Simonson Definition, 1981

Unit lacks or shares complete plumbing facilities.

Unit lacks adequate provision for sewage disposal. The unit must be connected with a public sewer, septic tank, cesspool, or chemical toilet.

Unit lacks or shares complete kitchen facilities.

Has three or more structural problems:

> Leaking roof.
> Open cracks or holes in interior walls or ceiling.
> Holes in the interior floors.
> Peeling paint or broken plaster over one square foot on an interior wall.
> Evidence of mice or rats in last 90 days.

Has three or more common area problems:

> No working light fixtures in common hallway.
> Loose, broken, or missing stairs.
> Broken or missing stair railings.
> No elevator in building (for units two or more floors from main building entrance in building four or more stories high).

Unit is heated mainly by unvented room heaters which burn gas, oil, or kerosene.

Lacks electricity.

Has three signs of electrical inadequacy:

> One or more rooms without a working wall outlet.
> Fuses blown or circuit breakers tripped three or more times during last 90 days.
> Exposed wiring in house.

Source: Simonson, J. 1981. Measuring Inadequate Housing through the Use of the Annual Housing Survey, Washington, D.C.: Office of Policy Development and Research, U.S. Department of Housing and Urban Development, pp. 84-85.

HUD's Restricted Definitions

Unit is "severely inadequate" if it exhibits one or more of the following flaws:

Lacks or shares complete plumbing facilities.

Contains five of the following six signs of inadequate maintenance:

>Leaking roof.
>Open cracks or holes in interior walls and ceilings.
>Holes in the interior floors.
>Peeling paint or broken plaster over one square foot on an interior wall.
>Evidence of mice or rats in last 90 days.
>Leaks in basement. (For units without basements, four of five signs.)

Contains four or more of the following public hall deficiencies:

>No working light fixtures in public halls.
>Loose, broken, or missing steps on common stairways.
>Loose or missing stair railings.
>No elevator in the building (for units two or more floors from main building entrance in four or more story building).

Heating equipment breakdown of six consecutive hours or longer three or more times last winter.

Experiences three selected electrical defects or no electricity:

>Lacks working electrical wall outlet in one or more rooms.
>Blown fuses or tripped circuit breakers three or more times in the last 90 days.
>Exposed wiring.

Inadequate provision for sewage disposal. Adequate means of sewage disposal include a public sewer, septic tank, cesspool, or chemical toilet. Facilities must be in the structure.

Source: An Analysis of the Housing Needs of New York State: Research Design. Exhibit E.2. March 1983. Cambridge, MA: Department of Housing and Urban Development, Office of Policy Development, and Research and Urban Systems Research and Engineering, Inc.

Elderly Housing 1

Unit lacks or shares complete plumbing facilities.

Unit lacks or shares complete kitchen facilities.

One or more of the following three services was unavailable or completely unusable for six or more hours at least three times during the past ninety days: (1) running water, (2) sewage system, (3) toilet.

The heating system was completely unusable for six or more hours at least three times during the past winter.

Two or more of the following four conditions exist:

Leaking roof.
Substantial cracks or holes in walls and ceilings.
Holes in floors.
Broken plaster or peeling paint over one square foot on interior walls.

The unit is in a building with public hallways and stairs, and two or more of the following three conditions exists:

Missing light fixtures.
Stair railings are missing or poorly attached.
Missing, loose, or broken steps.

Source: Struyk, Raymond and Beth Soldo. 1980. Improving the Elderly's Housing: A Key to Preserving the Nation's Housing Stock and Neighborhoods. Cambridge, MA: Ballinger Publishing.

Congressional Budget Office, 1978

A unit fails if it has one or more major deficiency or two or more secondary deficiencies.

The major deficiencies are:

> The absence of complete plumbing facilities.
> The absence of complete kitchen facilities.
> The absence of a public sewer connection, septic tank, or cesspool.
> Three or more breakdowns of six or more hours each time in the sewer, septic tank, or cesspool during the prior 90 days.
> Three or more breakdowns of six or more hours each time in the heating system during the last winter.
> Three or more times completely without water for six or more hours each time during the prior 90 days.
> Three or more times completely without a flush toilet for six or more hours each time during the prior 90 days.

Secondary deficiencies are:

> Leaking roof.
> Holes in interior floors.
> Open cracks or holes in interior walls or ceilings.
> Broken plaster (over one square foot in area) on interior walls or ceilings.
> Exposed wiring.
> The absence of any working light in public hallways.
> Loose or missing handrails in public hallways.
> Loose, broken, or missing steps in public hallways.

Source: Congressional Budget Office. 1978. Federal Housing Policy: Current Programs and Recurring Issues. Background paper of the U.S. Congress. Table 1, fn. b, p. 6. Washington, D.C.

Welfare and Housing

Unit lacks or shares complete plumbing facilities.

Unit lacks adequate provision for sewage disposal. The unit must be connected with a public sewer, septic tank, cesspool, or chemical toilet.

Unit lacks or shares complete kitchen facilities.

Has two or more structural problems:

> Leaking roof.
> Leaking basement.
> Open cracks or holes in interior walls or ceilings.
> Holes in the interior floors.
> Peeling paint or broken plaster over one square foot on an interior wall.
> Evidence of mice or rats in last 90 days.

Has two or more common area problems:

> No working light fixture in common hallway.
> Loose, broken, or missing stairs.
> Broken or missing stair railings.
> No elevator in building (for units two or more floors from main building entrance in building four or more stories high).

Unit is heated mainly by unvented room heaters which burn gas, oil, or kerosense.

Unit has had three or more toilet breakdowns of six hours or more in the past 90 days.

Unit had three or more heating breakdowns lasting six hours or more last winter.

Lacks electricity.

One or more rooms without a working wall outlet.

Fuses blown or circuit breakers tripped three or more times during last 90 days.

Exposed wiring in house.

Source: Definition used in current paper.

Elderly Housing 2

Unit lacks or shares complete plumbing facilities.

Unit lacks or shares complete kitchen facilities.

Unit lacks adequate provision for sewage disposal. Unit must be connected with a public sewer, septic tank, cesspool, or chemical toilet.

Basement leaks.

No elevator in building (for units two or more floors from the main building entrance in buildings four or more stories high).

Unit heated mainly by unvented room heaters which burn gas, oil, or kerosene.

Lacks electricity.

Unit lacks a working electrical wall outlet in one or more rooms.

Source: Zais, James, Raymond J. Struyk, and Thomas Thibodeau. Housing Assistance for Older Americans. Washington, D.C.: The Urban Institute, p. 32.

HUD's Extended Definition

Unit is "potentially inadequate" if it has one or more of the following flaws:

Unit lacks or shares complete plumbing facilities.

Unit lacks or shares complete kitchen facilities.

Unit shows three of six signs of inadequate maintenance:

> Leaking roof.
> Open cracks or holes in interior walls and ceilings.
> Holes in the interior floors.
> Peeling paint or broken plaster over one square foot on an interior wall.
> Evidence of mice or rats in last 90 days.
> Leaks in basement.

Contains three or more public hall deficiencies:

> No light fixtures in public halls.
> Loose, broken, or missing steps on common stairways.
> Loose or missing stair railings.
> No elevator in the building (for units two or more floors from main building entrance in a building with four or more floors).

Unit lacks heating equipment, or unit is heated primarily by room heaters without flue or vent which burn gas, oil, or kerosene.

Heating equipment breakdown of six consecutive hours or longer three or more times last winter.

Experiences three selected electrical defects or no electricity:

> Lacks working electrical wall outlet in one or more rooms.
> Blown fuses or tripped circuit breakers three or more times in the last 90 days.
> Exposed wiring.

Inadequate provision for sewage disposal and/or break down of the facilities. Adequate means of sewage disposal include a public sewer, septic tank, cesspool, or chemical toilet. Facilities must be in the structure. Breakdown of flush toilet six consecutive hours or longer, three or more times during the last 90 days.

Source: An Analysis of the Housing Needs of New York State: Research Design. March 1983. Exhibit E-1. Cambridge, MA: U.S. Department of Housing and Urban Development, Office of Policy Development and Research, and Urban Systems Research and Engineering, Inc.

New York State Study

A unit fails if it has one or more major deficiency or two or more secondary deficiencies.

The major deficiencies are:

> The absence of complete plumbing facilities.[a]
> The absence of complete kitchen facilities.[b]
> No central heat.

Secondary deficiencies are:

> Leaking roof.
> Holes in interior floors.
> Open cracks or holes in interior walls or ceilings.
> Broken plaster (over one square foot) in area on interior walls or ceilings.
> Exposed wiring.
> The absence of any working light in public hallways.
> Loose or missing handrails in public hallways.
> Loose, broken, or missing steps in public hallways.

Source: An Analysis of the Housing Needs of New York State: Research Design. March 1983. Cambridge, MA: U.S. Department of Housing and Urban Development, Office of Policy Development and Research, and Urban Systems Research and Engineering, Inc., pp. 2-17.

a. Complete plumbing facilities: this requires a unit to have hot and cold piped water, a flush toilet, and a bathtub or shower all inside the structure.
b. Complete kitchen facilities: a unit must have an installed sink with piped water, a range or cook-stove, and a mechanical refrigerator all inside the structure.

The Office of Management and Budget, 1977

Any one or more of the following criteria cause a unit to fail:

Unit lacks or shares complete plumbing facilities.

Unit lacks or shares complete kitchen facilities.

Unit was completely without running water for six or more hours at least three times in the past 90 days.

Unit had completely unusable toilet for six hours at least three times in the past 90 days.

Unit had completely unusable sewage disposal system for six or more hours at least three times in the past 90 days.

Unit heated by unvented room heaters burning gas, oil, or kerosene.

Room(s) closed for a week or more during past winter because they could not be heated.

Completely unusable heating system for six or more hours three or more times during past winter.

Unit lacks a working electrical wall outlet in one or more rooms.

Leaking roof.

Cracks or holes in interior walls or ceiling.

Holes in floor.

Broken plaster or peeling paint (over one square foot) on interior walls.

Public halls lack working light fixtures.

Loose, broken, or missing steps on common stairways.

Not all stair railing firmly attached, or stair railings missing.

Evidence or rats or mice in last 90 days.

Source: Sunshine, Jonathan. "Memorandum for Distribution: Preliminary Findings of Section 8 Study--Report No. 8: Econometric Analysis of Contractor Data." 22 December 1977. Washington, D.C.: Office of Management and Budget, Special Studies Division, Human Resources, Veterans, and Labor.

Fair Market Rent

Any one of the following criteria causes a unit to fail:

Unit lacks complete plumbing facilities.

Unit lacks or shares complete kitchen facilities.

Stove, refrigerator, or sink not working.

Unit without running water for at least six hours at least three times in previous 90 days.

Completely unusuable toilet for at least six hours at least three times in previous 90 days.

Completely unusable sewage disposal for at least six hours at least three times in previous 90 days.

Heated by fireplace, stove, space heater, or by unvented room heaters burning gas, oil, or kerosene.

Rooms closed for a week or more during the past winter because they could not be heated.

Unusable heating system for at least six hours at least three times during the past winter.

Leaking roof.

Open cracks or holes in interior walls or ceiling.

Holes in the interior floor.

Broken plaster or peeling paint (over one square foot) on interior walls.

Public halls lack working light fixtures.

Loose or missing steps on common stairways.

Stair railings missing or not firmly attached.

Signs that rats or mice were present in the last 90 days.

Unit lacks direct access; entry is through another unit.

Unit lacks electricity.

Exposed wiring.

Fuses or circuit breakers blew three or more times in the last 90 days.

Unit lacks working electrical wall outlet in one or more rooms.

Source: Federal Register, various issues.

Crowding

Independent variables	All households			Renters		
	Elderly	Households with child(ren)	Other nonelderly	Elderly	Households with child(ren)	Other nonelderly
Constant	.26	.45**	.36**	.22**	.43**	.33**
Own	-.08	-.11**	-.13**			
Whether white	-.06*	-.11**	-.08**	-.03	-.06**	-.09**
Whether black	-.04	-.07**	-.09**	-.03	.01	.04
Central city	.01	.01	.00	.05	-.02	.02
Rest of SMSA	-.01	-.00	-.02	.02		
Household size	.16**	.15**	.16**	.16**	.15**	.16**
Income	-.00**	-.00**	-.00**	-.00	-.00**	-.00**
Northeast	.01	-.02	.00	.02	-.01	-.00
North Central	.00	-.05**	-.03	-.03	-.03*	-.02
West	.02	.05**	.03	.05	.05*	.05
Whether female head	.11**	-.04**			-.04*	
Housing asst. only	.04	-.06**	-.05*	.10**	-.05**	-.05*
Both housing & welfare		-.07**	-.07**	.03	-.07**	-.07*
$\overline{R}^2$ (adj.)	.54	.48	.59	.45	.51	.52
(N)	551	2,273	901	246	1,808	522

Source: 1983 American Housing Survey

1. Crowding is measured by persons per room.
2. Restricted to households with two or more persons.
3. Renters exclude households who neither own nor rent.

* Significant at .05 level.
** Significant at .01 level.

Appendix F (continued)

Affordability

Independent variables	All households			Renters		
	Elderly	Households with child(ren)	Other nonelderly	Elderly	Households with child(ren)	Other nonelderly
Constant	41.25**	68.47**	57.11**	48.14**	76.20**	63.23**
Own	-2.40	-.50	-.11	2.60	1.75	-.15
Whether white	.65	2.05	-.56	.48	-.49	.16
Whether black	-1.35	.52	1.28			
Central city	7.92**	5.71**	5.40**	6.13**	3.87**	5.60**
Rest of SMSA	3.72*	7.43**	8.16**	4.35**	5.69**	10.64**
Household size	.16	-1.33**	-.16	.09	-1.14**	.03
Income	-.00**	-.00**	-.00**	-.00**	-.00**	-.00**
Northeast	4.50*	3.51*	5.65**	4.56**	.49	5.79**
North Central	3.51*	3.18*	5.80**	3.32*	.56	5.50**
West	3.13	.83	2.95	3.64	-.45	4.80*
Whether female head		4.58**			3.85**	
Housing asst. only	-9.91**	-21.09**	-17.12**	-14.03**	-20.70**	-16.42**
Both housing & welfare	-8.98**	-18.11**	-14.84**	-14.17**	-18.53**	-17.93**
$\overline{R}^2$ (adj.)	.09	.37	.25	.21	.44	.41
(N)	1,344	2,204	1,338	930	1,784	940

Source: 1983 American Housing Survey.

1. Affordability measured by annual housing costs divided by income.

* Significant at .05 level.
** Significant at .01 level.

Appendix F (continued)

Housing Quality

Independent variables	All households			Renters		
	Elderly	Households with child(ren)	Other nonelderly	Elderly	Households with child(ren)	Other nonelderly
Constant	1.61**	.98**	1.39**	1.52**	.96**	1.31**
Own	-.34**	-.21**	-.31**			
Whether white	-.21	-.17*	-.11	-.28*	-.19*	-.19
Whether black	.29*	.16*	.20*	.18	.15	.17
Central city	-.19*	-.12	-.10	-.11	-.09	.00
Rest of SMSA	-.02	-.14*	-.23**	-.02	-.16*	-.16
Household size	.14**	.09**	.03	.14**	.08**	.03
Income	-.00**	-.00**	-.00**	-.00**	-.00	-.00**
Northeast	-.34**	.23**	-.00	-.25**	.25**	.06
North Central	-.35**	-.21**	-.31**	-.30**	-.28**	-.25*
West	-.49**	-.33**	-.39**	-.40**	-.40**	-.33**
Whether female head		.08			.11	
Housing asst. only	-.89**	-.62**	-.85**	-.87**	-.64**	-.80**
Both housing & welfare	-1.01**	-.54**	-.66**	-.97**	-.52**	-.64**
$\overline{R}^2$ (adj.)	.26	.11	.13	.29	.12	.14
(N)	1,344	2,204	1,338	930	1,784	940

Source: 1983 National American Housing Survey.

1. Housing quality measured as a count of physical housing deficiencies.

 * Significant at .05 level.
** Significant at .01 level.

PART 2 DATA

5

AID TO FAMILIES WITH DEPENDENT CHILDREN

Aid to Families with Dependent Children (AFDC), the largest income assistance program, was created to enable each state and jurisdiction to provide a minimum standard of living to needy dependent children and, in some cases, to their caretakers. The Department of Health and Human Services and state public assistance departments jointly administer AFDC in accordance with the unrestricted money payment principle of the Social Security Act of 1935 (Public Law 74-271). By law, the government may not control how recipients use their grant.

The federal government has established general guidelines for the program but remains silent on the question of what constitutes a minimum standard of living and which items (food, shelter, clothing, and so on) are to be included in a state's standard of need. Each state is responsible for defining its standard of need and payment level as it sees fit.[1] Although not required, each state has included shelter in its standard of need since the program's inception.[2]

The following tables provide a state-by-state description of the treatment of shelter under AFDC. Table 5.1 shows each state's standard of need, shelter need, ratio of shelter need to standard of need, payment level, and shelter payment for families with one to six members.[3] It reflects the situation that existed as of 1984 or 1985 (depending on when the state was interviewed). Table 5.2 shows, for each state, the average monthly caseload, average number of recipients, and average family size for fiscal 1983.[4] It also provides three estimates of total shelter expenditures based on fiscal 1983 total expenditures for AFDC benefits. Table 5.3 contains five separate parts. For each state, these tables compare the standard of need, shelter need, ratio of shelter need to standard of need, payment level, and shelter payment for families with three and four members. Table 5.4 lists the federal share of AFDC by state for 1984-85. Table 5.5 shows selected household characteristics of AFDC recipients, by state, for 1984.

Data for tables 5.1 through 5.3 were collected through telephone interviews with each state's public assistance department and from supporting state documents. Tables 5.4 and 5.5 are based on data in government publications.

ORGANIZATION

The states are divided into three categories depending upon how easily we could estimate the proportion of the welfare grant that is allocated to shelter.

1. **Explicit**--The state has a published shelter component included in its standard of need and payment standard or it has a specific line item for shelter costs in its aggregate AFDC fiscal year budget.

2. **Derived**--Various pieces of information can be used to estimate the shelter need amount. In some instances, a different overall standard of need (and payment level) is established for recipients who have no housing costs; here, shelter needs and payment levels can be derived by comparing the grants available to such recipients to the grants available to families who must pay for housing. In other cases, states were able to give us a rough percentage of the standard of need and payment level devoted to shelter.

3. **Fully consolidated**--The ratio of shelter need to standard of need has been set at 30 percent because the state's shelter need is neither explicit nor derivable. The 30 percent is based upon the amount of income a family is expected to spend on rent in subsidized housing. Further, it represents a rough average of the states with either explicit or derived shelter assistance components.

Notes

1. Based on Title IV-A of the Social Security Act of 1935 (PL 74-271), as amended, 1985, and AFDC chapter in <u>Background Material and Data on Programs within the Jurisdiction of the Committee on Ways and Means</u>, Committee Print WMCP 99-2, 99 Cong., 1 sess. Washington, D.C. February 1985. Standard of need is defined as the state's estimate of how much it costs a family to maintain a minimum standard of living. Payment level is the maximum dollar amount the state provides to a family.

2.   Conversation with Wilbur Cohen, former Secretary of the Department of Health, Education, and Welfare. Spring 1985.

3.   Shelter need is the state's estimate of how much it costs for a family to secure shelter; shelter payment is the maximum dollar amount the state provides to a family for shelter.

4.   State fiscal years do not necessarily correspond to the federal fiscal year. For example, state fiscal 1983 was usually defined as July 1982 to June 1983. A majority of the aggregate AFDC data reflect state fiscal 1983.

Table 5.1   AFDC TOTAL AND SHELTER BENEFIT STANDARDS AND
PAYMENTS, BY FAMILY SIZE, 1983-84[a]
(dollars unless otherwise indicated)

State and measure	Family size (number of persons)					
	One	Two	Three	Four	Five	Six
Arkansas						
Standard of need	97	193	234	273	310	345
Shelter need	20	40	40	40	40	40
Ratio of shelter need to standard of need (percent)[b]	20.6	20.7	17.8	14.7	12.9	11.6
Payment level	58	116	140	164	186	207
Shelter payment[c]	12	24	24	24	24	24
California						
Standard of need	272	448	558	660	753	847
Shelter need	148	194	211	222	222	222
Ratio of shelter need to standard of need (percent)[b]	54.4	43.3	37.8	33.6	29.5	26.2
Payment level	272	448	558	660	753	847
Shelter payment	148	194	211	222	222	222
Connecticut: Region A						
Standard of need	346	440	546	636	718	802
Shelter need	206	206	237	265	272	280
Ratio of shelter need to standard of need (percent)[b]	59.5	46.8	43.4	41.6	37.9	34.9
Payment level	346	440	546	636	718	802
Shelter payment	206	206	237	265	272	280
Connecticut: Region B						
Standard of need	286	380	467	549	628	710
Shelter need	146	146	159	177	182	187
Ratio of shelter need to standard of need (percent)[b]	51.0	38.4	34.0	32.2	28.9	26.3
Payment level	286	380	467	549	615	710
Shelter payment	146	146	159	177	182	187

Table 5.1 (continued)

State and measure	Family size (number of persons)					
	One	Two	Three	Four	Five	Six
Connecticut: Region C						
Standard of need	286	380	460	534	608	690
Shelter need	146	146	152	162	162	168
Ratio of shelter need to standard of need (percent)[b]	51.0	38.4	33.0	30.0	26.6	24.3
Payment level	286	380	460	534	608	690
Shelter payment	146	146	152	162	162	168
Hawaii						
Standard of need	297	319	468	546	626	709
Shelter need	175	215	240	265	290	320
Ratio of shelter need to standard of need (percent)[b]	58.9	67.4	51.3	48.5	46.3	45.1
Payment level	297	319	468	546	626	709
Shelter payment	175	215	240	265	290	320
Idaho						
Standard of need	365	446	554	627	700	760
Shelter need	117	117	142	142	142	142
Ratio of shelter need to standard of need (percent)[b]	32.1	26.2	25.6	22.6	20.3	18.7
Payment level	201	245	304	344	385	418
Shelter payment	65	66	78	78	78	78
Illinois: Group I - Chicago						
Standard of need	381	480	657	742	867	974
Shelter need[d]	198	235	304	297	361	385
Ratio of shelter need to standard of need (percent)[b]	52.0	48.9	46.2	40.1	41.6	39.5
Payment level	198	250	342	386	451	506
Shelter payment[e]	103	122	158	155	187	200
Indiana						
Standard of need	195	255	315	375	435	495
Shelter need	100	100	100	100	100	100
Ratio of shelter need to standard of need (percent)[b]	51.3	39.2	31.7	26.7	22.9	20.2
Payment level	98	196	256	316	376	436
Shelter payment	50	77	81	84	86	88

Table 5.1 (continued)

State and measure	Family size (number of persons)					
	One	Two	Three	Four	Five	Six
Iowa						
Standard of need	213	421	497	578	640	712
Shelter need	44	92	93	100	102	104
Ratio of shelter need to standard of need (percent)[b]	20.6	21.7	18.7	17.2	15.9	14.6
Payment level	154	305	360	419	464	516
Shelter payment	32	66	67	72	74	75
Kansas: Group I[f]						
Standard of need	189	255	314	363	406	449
Shelter need	76	76	76	76	76	76
Ratio of shelter need to standard of need (percent)[b]	40.2	29.8	24.2	20.9	18.7	16.9
Payment level	189	255	314	363	406	449
Shelter payment	76	76	76	76	76	76
Kansas: Group V[e]						
Standard of need	248	314	373	422	465	508
Shelter need	135	135	135	135	135	135
Ratio of shelter need to standard of need (percent)[b]	54.4	43.0	36.2	32.0	29.0	26.6
Payment level	248	314	373	422	465	508
Shelter payment	135	135	135	135	135	135
Maine						
Standard of need	239	379	510	641	772	903
Shelter need	80	127	170	214	257	300
Ratio of shelter need to standard of need (percent)[b]	33.4	33.5	33.3	33.4	33.3	33.2
Payment level	174	275	370	465	560	665
Shelter payment[c]	58	92	123	155	186	221
Maryland						
Standard of need	192	337	433	520	603	665
Shelter need	71	124	159	191	222	245
Ratio of shelter need to standard of need (percent)[b]	36.8	36.8	36.8	36.8	36.8	36.8
Payment level	139	224	313	376	436	481
Shelter payment[b]	51	82	115	138	160	177

Table 5.1 (continued)

State and measure	Family size (number of persons)					
	One	Two	Three	Four	Five	Six
Michigan: Zone I, Area I (low)						
Standard of need	273	370	459	564	659	846
Shelter need	95	105	115	140	150	195
Ratio of shelter need to standard of need (percent)[b]	34.8	28.4	25.1	24.8	22.8	23.0
Payment level	250	339	420	516	603	774
Shelter payment	95	105	115	140	150	195
Michigan: Zone II, Area VI (high)						
Standard of need	338	435	523	628	723	862
Shelter need	150	160	170	195	205	250
Ratio of shelter need to standard of need (percent)[b]	44.4	36.8	32.5	31.1	28.4	29.0
Payment level	309	398	479	575	662	789
Shelter payment	150	160	170	195	205	250
Mississippi						
Standard of need	171	244	286	327	360	391
Shelter need	60	60	60	60	60	60
Ratio of shelter need to standard of need (percent)[b]	35.1	24.5	21.0	18.3	16.7	15.3
Payment level	0	60	96	120	144	168
Shelter payment[c]	0	15	20	22	24	26
Nebraska						
Standard of need	210	280	359	420	490	560
Shelter need	101	101	103	105	108	109
Ratio of shelter need to standard of need (percent)[b]	48.1	36.1	29.9	25.0	22.0	19.4
Payment level	210	280	350	420	490	560
Shelter payment[c]	101	101	103	105	108	109
New Hampshire: Regular housing (high)						
Standard of need	271	329	389	442	493	561
Shelter need	141	141	141	141	141	141
Ratio of shelter need to standard of need (percent)[b]	52.0	42.9	36.2	32.0	38.6	25.1
Payment level	271	329	389	442	493	561
Shelter payment	141	141	141	141	141	141

Table 5.1 (continued)

State and measure	Family size (number of persons)					
	One	Two	Three	Four	Five	Six
New Hampshire: Subsidized housing (low)						
Standard of need	271	313	367	418	470	535
Shelter need	174	174	174	174	174	174
Ratio of shelter need to standard of need (percent)[b]	62.4	55.6	47.4	41.6	37.0	32.5
Payment level	271	313	367	418	470	535
Shelter payment	174	174	174	174	174	174
New Mexico						
Standard of need	145	210	258	313	359	391
Shelter need	88	88	88	105	105	105
Ratio of shelter need to standard of need (percent)[b]	60.7	41.9	34.1	33.5	29.2	26.9
Payment level	145	210	258	313	359	391
Shelter payment	88	88	88	105	105	105
New York: New York City						
Standard of need	287	377	444	528	599	676
Shelter need	193	227	244	270	281	308
Ratio of shelter need to standard of need (percent)[b]	67.2	60.2	55.0	51.1	46.9	45.6
Payment level	287	377	444	528	599	676
Shelter payment	193	227	244	270	281	308
New York: Erie County						
Standard of need	248	333	393	457	524	578
Shelter need	154	183	193	199	206	210
Ratio of shelter need to standard of need (percent)[b]	62.1	55.0	49.1	43.5	39.3	36.3
Payment level	248	333	393	457	524	578
Shelter payment	154	183	193	199	206	210

Note: Because there is much variation across the state by county, we chose New York City and the most populous upstate county, Erie.

Oregon						
Standard of need	182	252	310	392	474	550
Shelter need	77	98	116	140	165	188
Ratio of shelter need to standard of need (percent)[b]	42.5	39.0	37.4	35.8	34.8	34.1
Payment level	182	252	310	392	474	550
Shelter payment	77	98	116	140	165	188

Table 5.1 (continued)

State and measure	Family size (number of persons)					
	One	Two	Three	Four	Five	Six
South Carolina						
Standard of need	102	144	187	229	272	314
Shelter need	44	44	44	44	44	44
Ratio of shelter need to standard of need (percent)[b]	43.1	30.6	23.5	19.2	16.2	14.0
Payment level	102	144	187	229	272	314
Shelter payment	44	44	44	44	44	44
South Dakota						
Standard of need	220	286	329	371	413	455
Shelter need	163	163	163	163	163	163
Ratio of shelter need to standard of need (percent)[b]	74.1	57.0	49.5	43.9	39.5	35.8
Payment level	220	286	329	371	413	455
Shelter payment	163	163	163	163	163	163
Tennessee						
Standard of need	126	189	246	300	351	405
Shelter need[d]	38	57	74	90	106	122
Ratio of shelter need to standard of need (percent)[b]	30.1	30.1	30.1	30.1	30.1	30.1
Payment level[c]	71	106	138	168	197	227
Shelter payment	21	32	42	51	59	68
Texas						
Standard of need	205	425	494	593	661	760
Shelter need	83	166	166	188	188	209
Ratio of shelter need to standard of need (percent)[b]	40.4	39.0	33.7	31.8	28.5	27.5
Payment level	69	144	167	201	224	258
Shelter payment[e]	28	56	56	64	64	71
Utah						
Standard of need	401	556	693	809	992	1,014
Shelter need	191	235	276	297	321	318
Ratio of shelter need to standard of need (percent)[b]	47.6	42.3	39.8	36.7	32.4	31.4
Payment level	212	294	367	428	488	537
Shelter payment[c]	101	124	146	157	158	169

Table 5.1 (continued)

State and measure	Family size (number of persons)					
	One	Two	Three	Four	Five	Six
Vermont						
Standard of Need	482	586	699	798	910	980
Shelter need	263	263	263	263	263	263
Ratio of shelter need to standard of need (percent)[b]	54.7	44.9	37.6	33.0	29.0	26.8
Payment level	316	384	458	523	596	642
Shelter payment	173	173	173	173	173	173

Note: The standard of need includes basic need plus shelter need minus fuel costs, which, when furnished, are deducted from the standard of need. The shelter need is the maximum.

Virginia: Group I						
Standard of need	135	212	273	331	390	437
Shelter need	71	108	125	141	164	177
Ratio of shelter need to standard of need (percent)[b]	52.9	50.9	45.7	42.6	42.0	40.5
Payment level	121	191	245	298	351	394
Shelter payment	64	97	112	127	147	160
Virginia: Group II						
Standard of need	161	238	298	357	422	470
Shelter need	92	132	150	168	195	210
Ratio of shelter need to standard of need (percent)[b]	57.4	55.5	50.2	47.1	46.3	44.6
Payment level	145	214	269	321	379	423
Shelter payment	83	119	135	151	176	189
Virginia: Group III						
Standard of need	225	302	363	422	501	548
Shelter need	136	176	192	210	246	259
Ratio of shelter need to standard of need (percent)[b]	60.2	58.4	53.0	49.8	49.0	47.3
Payment level	203	272	327	379	451	493
Shelter payment	122	159	173	189	221	233

Table 5.1 (continued)

State and measure	Family size (number of persons)					
	One	Two	Three	Four	Five	Six
West Virginia: Plan III (high)						
Standard of need	161	216	275	332	379	429
Shelter need	59	57	57	63	63	69
Ratio of shelter need to standard of need (percent)[b]	36.4	26.2	20.9	18.9	16.5	16.1
Payment level	121	164	206	249	284*	322*
Shelter payment	44	43	43	47	47	52

*Maximum payment is $275.

State and measure	One	Two	Three	Four	Five	Six
West Virginia: Plan I (low)						
Standard of need	72	130	186	238	285	329
Shelter need	0	0	0	0	0	0
Ratio of shelter need to standard of need (percent)[b]	0.0	0.0	0.0	0.0	0.0	0.0
Payment level	54	98	140	179	214	247
Shelter payment	0	0	0	0	0	0
Arizona						
Standard of need	130	180	233	282	322	360
Shelter need	52	72	93	112	128	143
Ratio of shelter need to standard of need (percent)	39.7	39.7	39.7	39.7	39.7	39.7
Payment level	130	180	233	282	322	360
Shelter payment[e]	52	72	93	112	128	143
Colorado						
Standard of need	253	496	631	765	907	1,045
Shelter need[c]	68	134	170	207	245	282
Ratio of shelter need to standard of need (percent)	27.0	27.0	27.0	27.0	27.0	27.0
Payment level	208	272	346	420	498	574
Shelter payment[e]	56	73	93	113	135	155
Delaware						
Standard of need	152	212	287	336	416	475
Shelter need[c]	46	64	86	101	125	143
Ratio of shelter need to standard of need (percent)	30.0	30.0	30.0	30.0	30.0	30.0
Payment level	152	212	287	336	416	475
Shelter payment[e]	46	64	86	101	125	143

Table 5.1 (continued)

State and measure	Family size (number of persons)					
	One	Two	Three	Four	Five	Six
Florida: Standard with shelter allowance						
Standard of need	221	297	400	468	549	618
Shelter need[g]	95	95	135	135	160	160
Ratio of shelter need to standard of need (percent)[h]	43.0	32.0	33.8	28.8	29.1	25.9
Payment level	137	185	240	284	328	370
Shelter payment	59	59	81	82	96	96
Florida: Standard without shelter allowance						
Standard of need	126	202	265	333	389	458
Shelter need	0	0	0	0	0	0
Ratio of shelter need to standard of need (percent)[b]	0.0	0.0	0.0	0.0	0.0	0.0
Payment level	77	126	158	202	231	275
Shelter payment	0	0	0	0	0	0
Massachusetts						
Standard of need	273	347	418	490	562	635
Shelter need	125	125	125	125	125	125
Ratio of shelter need to standard of need (percent)[b]	45.9	36.1	30.0	25.6	22.3	19.8
Payment level	258	328	396	463	531	600
Shelter payment[c]	118	118	119	119	122	119
Montana: Standard with shelter allowance						
Standard of need	256	337	401	513	607	682
Shelter need[g]	164	188	199	250	296	332
Ratio of shelter need to standard of need (percent)[h]	64.1	55.8	49.6	48.7	48.8	48.7
Payment level	212	279	332	425	501	564
Shelter payment[c]	136	156	165	207	245	275
Montana: Standard without shelter allowance						
Standard of need	92	149	202	263	311	350
Shelter need	0	0	0	0	0	0
Ratio of shelter need to standard of need (percent)	0.0	0.0	0.0	0.0	0.0	0.0
Payment level	76	123	167	217	258	290
Shelter payment	0	0	0	0	0	0

Table 5.1 (continued)

State and measure	Family size (number of persons)					
	One	Two	Three	Four	Five	Six
North Dakota						
Standard of need	201	301	371	454	516	569
Shelter need[d]	50	75	93	114	129	142
Ratio of shelter need to standard of need (percent)	25.0	25.0	25.0	25.0	25.0	25.0
Payment level	201	301	371	454	516	569
Shelter payment[e]	50	75	93	114	129	142
Washington: Standard with shelter allowance						
Standard of need	491	621	768	904	1,008	1,182
Shelter need[g]	310	358	420	471	490	579
Ratio of shelter need to standard of need (percent)[h]	63.1	57.6	54.7	52.1	48.6	49.0
Payment level	304	385	476	561	646	731
Shelter payment[c]	192	222	260	292	314	358
Washington: Standard without shelter allowance						
Standard of need	181	263	348	433	518	603
Shelter need	0	0	0	0	0	0
Ratio of shelter need to standard of need (percent)	0.0	0.0	0.0	0.0	0.0	0.0
Payment level	181	263	348	433	518	603
Shelter payment	0	0	0	0	0	0
Wyoming: Standard with shelter allowance						
Standard of need	195	320	360	390	450	510
Shelter need[g]	80	115	95	80	105	105
Ratio of shelter need to standard of need (percent)[h]	41.0	35.9	26.4	20.5	23.3	20.6
Payment level	195	320	360	390	450	510
Shelter payment	80	115	95	80	105	105
Wyoming: Standard without shelter allowance						
Standard of need	115	205	265	310	345	405
Shelter need	0	0	0	0	0	0
Ratio of shelter need to standard of need (percent)	0.0	0.0	0.0	0.0	0.0	0.0
Payment level	115	205	265	310	345	405
Shelter payment	0	0	0	0	0	0

Table 5.1 (continued)

State and measure	Family size (number of persons)					
	One	Two	Three	Four	Five	Six
Alabama						
Standard of need	192	288	384	480	576	672
Shelter need[1]	58	86	115	144	172	202
Ratio of shelter need to standard of need (percent)[1]	30.0	30.0	30.0	30.0	30.0	30.0
Payment level	59	88	118	147	177	206
Shelter payment[1]	18	26	35	44	53	62
Alaska						
Standard of need	254	638	719	800	881	962
Shelter need[1]	76	191	(216)	(240)	264	289
Ratio of shelter need to standard of need (percent)[1]	30.0	30.0	(30.0)	(30.0)	30.0	30.0
Payment level	254	638	719	800	881	962
Shelter payment[1]	76	191	(216)	(240)	264	289
District of Columbia						
Standard of need	412	514	654	798	920	1,080
Shelter need[1]	124	154	196	239	276	324
Ratio of shelter need to standard of need (percent)[1]	30.0	30.0	30.0	30.0	30.0	30.0
Payment level	206	257	327	399	460	540
Shelter payment[1]	62	77	98	120	138	162
Georgia						
Standard of need	202	306	366	432	494	536
Shelter need[1]	61	92	110	130	148	161
Ratio of shelter need to standard of need (percent)[h]	30.0	30.0	30.0	30.0	30.0	30.0
Payment level	123	187	223	264	301	327
Shelter payment[1]	37	56	67	79	90	98
Kentucky						
Standard of need	140	170	197	246	288	325
Shelter need[1]	42	51	59	74	86	98
Ratio of shelter need to standard of need (percent)[1]	30.0	30.0	30.0	30.0	30.0	30.0
Payment level	140	170	197	246	288	325
Shelter payment[1]	42	51	59	74	86	98

Table 5.1 (continued)

State and measure	Family size (number of persons)					
	One	Two	Three	Four	Five	Six
Louisiana: Region I - Non-urban						
Standard of need	200	373	528	658	783	899
Shelter need[1]	60	112	158	197	237	267
Ratio of shelter need to standard of need (percent)[1]	30.0	30.0	30.0	30.0	30.0	30.0
Payment level	66	123	174	217	259	296
Shelter payment[1]	20	37	52	65	78	89
Louisiana: Region II - Urban						
Standard of need	217	416	579	712	841	958
Shelter need[1]	65	125	174	214	252	287
Ratio of shelter need to standard of need (percent)[1]	30.0	30.0	30.0	30.0	30.0	30.0
Payment level	72	138	190	234	277	316
Shelter payment	22	41	57	70	83	95
Minnesota						
Standard of need	246	431	524	611	685	761
Shelter need[1]	74	129	157	183	206	228
Ratio of shelter need to standard of need (percent)[1]	30.0	30.0	30.0	30.0	30.0	30.0
Payment level	246	431	524	611	685	761
Shelter payment[1]	74	129	157	183	206	228
Missouri						
Standard of need	145	250	312	365	414	460
Shelter need[1]	44	75	94	110	124	138
Ratio of shelter need to standard of need (percent)[1]	30.0	30.0	30.0	30.0	30.0	30.0
Payment level	123	212	265	310	351	391
Shelter payment[1]	37	64	80	93	105	117
Nevada						
Standard of need	173	229	285	341	397	453
Shelter need[1]	52	69	86	102	119	136
Ratio of shelter need to standard of need (percent)[1]	30.0	30.0	30.0	30.0	30.0	30.0
Payment level	142	188	234	280	325	372
Shelter payment[1]	43	56	70	84	98	111

Table 5.1 (continued)

State and measure	Family size (number of persons)					
	One	Two	Three	Four	Five	Six
New Jersey						
Standard of need	217	288	381	443	486	569
Shelter need[1]	65	86	114	133	146	171
Ratio of shelter need to standard of need (percent)[1]	30.0	30.0	30.0	30.0	30.0	30.0
Payment level	217	288	381	443	486	569
Shelter payment[1]	65	86	114	133	146	171
North Carolina						
Standard of need	296	388	446	488	534	576
Shelter need[1]	89	116	134	146	160	173
Ratio of shelter need to standard of need (percent)[1]	30.0	30.0	30.0	30.0	30.0	30.0
Payment level	148	194	223	244	267	288
Shelter payment[1]	44	58	67	73	80	86
Ohio						
Standard of need	368	498	627	757	886	1,015
Shelter need[1]	110	149	188	227	266	305
Ratio of shelter need to standard of need (percent)[1]	30.0	30.0	30.0	30.0	30.0	30.0
Payment level	116	227	276	343	400	445
Shelter payment[1]	35	68	83	103	120	134
Oklahoma: Children and one or two adults included in the assistance payment						
Standard of need	--	218	282	349	409	468
Shelter need[1]	--	65	85	105	123	140
Ratio of shelter need to standard of need (percent)[1]	--	30.0	30.0	30.0	30.0	30.0
Payment level	--	218	282	349	409	468
Shelter payment[1]	--	65	85	105	123	140
Oklahoma: Children only (no adults) included in the assistance payment						
Standard of need	84	166	234	301	361	424
Shelter need[1]	25	50	70	90	108	127
Ratio of shelter need to standard of need (percent)[1]	30.0	30.0	30.0	30.0	30.0	30.0
Payment level	84	166	234	301	361	424
Shelter payment[1]	25	50	70	90	108	127

Table 5.1 (continued)

State and measure	Family size (number of persons)					
	One	Two	Three	Four	Five	Six
Pennsylvania						
Standard of need	298	461	587	724	859	976
Shelter need[1]	89	138	176	217	258	293
Ratio of shelter need to standard of need (percent)[1]	30.0	30.0	30.0	30.0	30.0	30.0
Payment level	177	273	348	429	509	578
Shelter payment[1]	53	82	104	129	153	173
Rhode Island						
Standard of need	251	343	424	484	544	613
Shelter need[1]	75	103	127	145	163	184
Ratio of shelter need to standard of need (percent)[1]	30.0	30.0	30.0	30.0	30.0	30.0
Payment level	251	343	424	484	544	613
Shelter payment[1]	75	103	127	145	163	184
Wisconsin: Area I						
Standard of need	302	534	628	749	860	930
Shelter need[1]	91	160	188	225	258	279
Ratio of shelter need to standard of need (percent)[1]	30.0	30.0	30.0	30.0	30.0	30.0
Payment level	257	454	534	637	731	791
Shelter payment[1]	77	136	160	191	219	237
Wisconsin: Area II						
Standard of need	292	518	608	723	835	902
Shelter need[1]	88	155	182	217	251	271
Ratio of shelter need to standard of need (percent)[1]	30.0	30.0	30.0	30.0	30.0	30.0
Payment level	248	440	517	618	710	767
Shelter payment[1]	74	132	155	185	213	230

Source: State documents and telephone interviews with state welfare officials.

a. State officials were interviewed in late 1984 and early 1985. The data reflect the standard of need and payment levels in effect at the time of the interview.
b. Derived by dividing the published shelter need by the published standard of need for each family size.

c. Derived by multiplying the published payment level by the shelter need/standard of need ratio for each family size.

d. Derived by multiplying the published standard of need by the published shelter need/standard of need ratio for each family size.

e. Derived by multiplying the published payment level by the published shelter need/standard of need ratio for each family size.

f. Shelter allowances have been established based on location in the state. There are five shelter groups in the state as follows: $76 for Group I, $86 for Group II, $97 for Group III, $109 for Group IV, and $135 for Group V. (Sec. 3322 of the Kansas Public Assistance Manual, Rev. 2, 1-85.)

If an AFDC assistance unit resides in a shared living arrangement, the assistance unit receives 100 percent of the basic allowance plus a percentage reduction of the shelter allowance of 60 percent for one, 50 percent for two, 40 percent for three, 35 percent for four, 30 percent for five, and 20 percent for six or more persons in the assistance unit. There are two exceptions: (1) the only person excluded from the assistance plan is an SSI recipient to whom the statutory one-third reduction has been applied to the SSI payment; or (2) there is a shared living arrangement resulting from a commercial and bona fide landlord-tenant relationship with persons excluded from the assistance plan (Sec. 3322.1 (2) and (3), and Sec. 3322.2 of the Kansas Public Assistance Manual, Rev. No. 2, 1-85).

g. Derived by subtracting the published standard of need without shelter assistance from the published standard of need with shelter assistance for each family size.

h. Derived by dividing the shelter need by the published standard of need.

i. The shelter need/standard of need ratio has been set at 30 percent since the state's shelter need is neither explicit nor derivable. The 30 percent is based upon the amount of income a family is expected to spend on rent in subsidized housing.

Table 5.2A AGGREGATE INFORMATION ON AFDC: CASELOADS, RECIPIENTS, AND EXPENDITURES, EXPLICIT DATA, 1983-84[a]

State	Average monthly caseload	Recipients monthly	Average family size	AFDC expenditures ($ million)	Shelter expenditures[b]		
					Uniform distribution ($ million)	National distribution ($ million)	State-specific distribution ($ million)
Arkansas	22,447	63,574	2.83	35,200,505	5,725,210	6,256,426	6,354,607
California	456,639	1,514,441	3.32	2,850,000,000	1,068,073,339	1,110,665,573	1,052,699,682
Connecticut	43,776	127,048	2.90	219,024,000	82,638,283	83,697,699	83,938,608
Hawaii	17,764	50,200	2.83	85,163,908	45,079,726	48,389,016	49,230,501
Idaho	6,823	18,544	2.72	21,192,191	5,140,420	5,307,201	5,383,043
Illinois	234,711	730,460	3.11	838,182,900	374,807,453	385,062,817	380,186,593
Indiana	56,496	167,696	2.97	144,579,180	46,289,666	48,585,719	48,212,550
Iowa	38,000	111,000	2.92	67,716,721	12,309,496	13,172,214	13,184,420
Kansas	23,906	69,494	2.91	88,151,473	27,328,533	28,170,810	28,274,982
Maine	18,500	62,000	3.35	55,000,000	18,352,900	18,375,024	18,353,040
Maryland	71,277	192,448	2.70	255,843,232	94,186,029	94,077,633	94,101,048
Michigan	239,848	750,914	3.13	1,109,160,000	333,614,923	335,248,912	328,668,463
Mississippi	50,957	148,482	2.91	55,524,252	12,124,411	12,229,911	12,259,207
Nebraska	14,003	40,910	2.92	53,614,508	16,093,319	16,719,609	16,743,495
New Hampshire	6,679	18,192	2.72	24,813,273	10,238,547	10,787,072	11,114,997
New Mexico	18,500	42,550	2.30	54,000,000	20,371,626	20,262,223	22,299,593
New York	361,009	1,081,264	3.00	1,743,769,000	888,415,016	923,210,762	917,242,079
Oregon	27,323	72,323	2.65	99,641,358	37,086,873	37,483,536	37,920,452

Table 5.2A (continued)

State	Average monthly caseload	Recipients monthly	Average family size	AFDC expenditures ($ million)	Shelter expenditures[b]		
					Uniform distribution ($ million)	National distribution ($ million)	State-specific distribution ($ million)
South Carolina	49,424	133,793	2.71	76,320,466	18,650,865	19,465,392	20,496,910
South Dakota	5,965	16,676	2.80	16,845,428	8,418,637	8,650,026	8,809,148
Tennessee	58,132	151,399	2.60	82,007,860	24,684,366	24,684,366	24,684,378
Texas	100,573	302,646	3.01	163,637,542	54,762,620	57,474,679	56,952,848
Utah	12,921	36,097	2.94	52,970,600	20,319,148	21,074,583	21,062,593
Vermont	8,370	24,827	2.97	37,823,695	14,232,128	14,898,980	14,811,269
Virginia	60,161	160,556	2.67	172,298,822	85,489,699	87,874,511	89,657,770
West Virginia	31,332	92,894	2.96	70,633,080	15,944,786	16,122,857	16,011,334
Total	2,034,906	6,180,428		8,473,113,994	3,340,378,019	3,447,947,551	3,378,653,609

Source: State documents and telephone interviews with state welfare officials.

a. The majority of data refer to state fiscal 1983 (July 1982 to June 1983). A smaller number of states reported data for calendar 1984, or federal fiscal 1983 (October 1982 to September 1983).

b. Expenditures resulting from applying three different distributions for family size. The uniform distribution assumes that family size is equally distributed over families with one to six members. The national distribution assumes that each state has a family size distribution identical to an estimated national distribution. The state-specific distribution, based on the national distribution, yields an expected family size in agreement with the average family size as displayed in the third column. The specific procedures used are described in greater detail in the appendix to this section.

Table 5.2B AGGREGATE INFORMATION ON AFDC: CASELOADS, RECIPIENTS, AND EXPENDITURES, DERIVED DATA, 1983-84[a]

State	Average monthly caseload	Recipients monthly	Average family size	AFDC expenditures ($ million)	Shelter expenditures[b]		
					Uniform distribution ($ million)	National distribution ($ million)	State-specific distribution ($ million)
Arizona	23,471	65,579	2.79	55,427,827	22,004,847	22,004,847	22,004,852
Colorado	29,989	67,372	2.25	101,460,468	27,394,326	27,394,326	27,394,355
Delaware	9,600	25,400	2.65	26,000,000	7,800,000	7,800,003	7,800,003
Florida	97,320	266,369	2.74	226,358,688	72,662,262	72,590,958	72,991,296
Massachusetts	87,533	245,825	2.81	452,300,000	135,050,857	141,691,718	144,685,901
Montana	6,312	17,263	2.73	22,412,613	11,790,995	11,730,369	11,909,944
North Dakota	3,953	10,815	2.74	14,740,951	3,685,238	3,685,238	3,685,239
Washington	58,341	158,978	2.72	241,002,600	130,611,585	132,886,102	134,339,912
Wyoming	2,763	7,161	2.59	10,331,324	2,889,093	3,026,585	3,269,208
Total	319,282	864,762		1,150,034,471	413,889,203	422,810,146	428,080,710

Source: State documents and telephone interviews with state welfare officals.

a. The majority of data refer to state fiscal 1983 (July 1982 to June 1983). A smaller number of states reported data for calendar 1984, or federal fiscal 1983 (October 1982 to September 1983).

b. Expenditures resulting from applying three different distributions for family size. The uniform distribution assumes that family size is equally distributed over families with one to six members. The national distribution assumes that each state has a family size distribution identical to an estimated national distribution. The state-specific distribution, based on the national distribution yields an expected family size in agreement with the average family size as displayed in the third column. The specific procedures used are described in greater detail in the appendix to this section.

Table 5.2C AGGREGATE INFORMATION ON AFDC: CASELOADS, RECIPIENTS AND EXPENDITURES, FULLY CONSOLIDATED DATA, 1983-84[a]

State	Average monthly caseload	Recipients monthly	Average family size	AFDC expenditures ($ million)	Shelter expenditures[b]		
					Uniform distribution ($ million)	National distribution ($ million)	State-specific distribution ($ million)
Alabama	54,926	154,426	2.81	$72,959,043	$21,887,713	$21,887,713	$21,887,717
Alaska	5,274	13,238	2.51	33,648,400	10,094,520	10,094,520	10,094,527
District of Columbia	22,000	72,000	3.27	72,000,000	21,600,000	21,600,000	21,599,988
Georgia	88,918	239,363	2.69	185,530,021	55,659,006	55,659,006	55,659,027
Kentucky	56,735	150,616	2.65	125,133,622	37,540,087	37,540,087	37,540,103
Louisiana	70,347	213,151	3.03	143,255,755	42,976,727	42,976,727	42,976,720
Minnesota	48,808	146,490	3.00	229,752,610	68,925,783	68,925,783	68,925,775
Missouri	67,000	190,000	2.84	200,000,000	60,000,000	60,000,000	60,000,009
Nevada	4,501	13,044	2.90	11,386,095	3,415,829	3,415,829	3,415,829
New Jersey	134,229	407,240	3.03	450,841,400	135,252,420	135,252,420	135,252,398
North Carolina	68,500	169,755	2.48	145,403,580	43,621,074	43,621,074	43,621,105
Ohio	217,090	652,651	3.01	682,489,973	204,746,992	204,746,992	204,746,967
Oklahoma	24,016	69,645	2.90	76,526,655	22,957,997	22,957,997	22,957,998
Pennsylvania	188,300	559,152	2.97	726,997,156	218,099,147	218,099,147	218,099,133
Rhode Island	15,951	45,282	2.84	68,128,555	20,438,567	20,438,567	20,438,569
Wisconsin	85,497	258,503	3.02	454,001,447	136,200,434	136,200,434	136,200,414
Total	1,152,092	3,354,556		$3,678,054,312	$1,103,416,296	$1,103,416,296	$1,103,416,278
National total	3,506,280	10,399,746		$13,301,202,777	$4,857,683,518	$4,974,173,993	$4,910,150,597

Source: State documents and telephone interviews with state welfare officals.

a. The majority of data refer to state fiscal 1983 (July 1982 to June 1983). A smaller number of states reported data for calendar 1984, or federal fiscal 1983 (October 1982 to September 1983).

b. Expenditures resulting from applying three different distributions for family size. The uniform distribution assumes that family size is equally distributed over families with one to six members. The national distribution assumes that each state has a family size distribution identical to an estimated national distribution. The state-specific distribution, based on the national distribution yields an expected family size in agreement with the average family size as displayed in the third column. The specific procedures used are described in greater detail in the appendix to this section.

Table 5.3A STANDARD OF NEED FOR FAMILY SIZES OF THREE AND FOUR
PERSONS, 1983-84 (dollars)

	Family size	
	---	---
State and subdivision	Three persons	Four persons
Alabama	384	480
Alaska	719	800
Arizona	233	282
Arkansas	234	273
California	558	660
Colorado	631	765
Connecticut: Region A (high)	546	636
Connecticut: Region C (low)	460	534
Delaware	287	336
District of Columbia	654	798
Florida	400	468
Georgia	366	432
Hawaii	468	546
Idaho	554	627
Illinois	657	752
Indiana	315	375
Iowa	497	578
Kansas: Group I (low)	314	363
Kansas: Group II (high)	373	422
Kentucky	197	246
Louisiana: Region I (low)	528	658
Louisiana: Region II (high)	579	712
Maine	510	640
Maryland	433	520
Massachusetts	418	490
Michigan: Zone I (low)	459	564
Michigan: Zone II (high)	523	628
Minnesota	524	611
Mississippi	286	327
Missouri	312	365
Montana	401	513
Nebraska	350	420

Table 5.3A (continued)

State and subdivision	Family size	
	Three persons	Four persons
Nevada	285	341
New Hampshire: Regular housing (high)	389	442
New Hampshire: Subsidized housing (low)	367	418
New Jersey	381	443
New Mexico	258	313
New York: New York City (high)	444	528
New York: Erie County (low)	393	457
North Carolina	446	488
North Dakota	371	454
Ohio	627	757
Oklahoma: Schedule A (high)	282	349
Oklahoma: Schedule B (low)	234	301
Oregon	310	392
Pennsylvania	587	724
Rhode Island	424	484
South Carolina	187	229
South Dakota	329	371
Tennessee	246	300
Texas	494	593
Utah	693	809
Vermont	699	798
Virginia: Group I (low)	273	331
Virginia: Group II (high)	363	422
Washington	768	904
West Virginia: Plan III (high)	275	332
West Virginia: Plan I (low)	186	236
Wisconsin: Area I (high)	628	749
Wisconsin: Area II (low)	608	723
Wyoming	360	390

Source: State documents and telephone interviews with state welfare officials.

Table 5.3B SHELTER NEED FOR FAMILY SIZES OF THREE AND FOUR
PERSONS, 1983-84[a] (dollars)

	Family size	
State and subdivision	Three persons	Four persons
Alabama	(115)	(144)
Alaska	(216)	(240)
Arizona	93	112
Arkansas	40	40
California	211	222
Colorado	170	207
Connecticut: Region I (high)	237	265
Connecticut: Region II (low)	152	162
Delaware	86	101
District of Columbia	196	239
Florida	135	135
Georgia	(110)	(130)
Hawaii	240	265
Idaho	142	142
Illinois	304	297
Indiana	100	100
Iowa	93	100
Kansas: Group I (low)	76	76
Kansas: Group II (high)	135	135
Kentucky	(59)	(74)
Louisiana: Region I (low)	(158)	(197)
Louisiana: Region II (high)	(174)	(214)
Maine	170	214
Maryland	159	191
Massachusetts	125	125
Michigan: Zone I (low)	115	140
Michigan: Zone II (high)	170	195
Minnesota	(157)	(183)
Mississippi	60	60
Missouri	(94)	(110)
Montana	199	250
Nebraska	103	105

Table 5.3B (continued)

	Family size	
State and subdivision	Three persons	Four persons
Nevada	(86)	(102)
New Hampshire: Regular housing (high)	141	141
New Hampshire: Subsidized housing (low)	174	174
New Jersey	(114)	(133)
New Mexico	88	105
New York: New York City (high)	244	270
New York: Erie County (low)	193	199
North Carolina	(134)	(146)
North Dakota	93	114
Ohio	(188)	(227)
Oklahoma: Schedule A (high)	(85)	(105)
Oklahoma: Schedule B (low)	(70)	(90)
Oregon	116	140
Pennsylvania	(176)	(217)
Rhode Island	(129)	(145)
South Carolina	44	44
South Dakota	163	163
Tennessee	57	74
Texas	165	188
Utah	276	297
Vermont	263	263
Virginia: Group I (low)	125	141
Virginia: Group III (high)	192	210
Washington	420	471
West Virginia: Plan III (high)	57	63
West Virginia: Plan I (low)	0	0
Wisconsin: Area I (high)	188	225
Wisconsin: Area II (low)	182	217
Wyoming	95	80

Source: State documents and telephone interviews with state welfare officials.

a. The numbers in parentheses are estimates for fully consolidated states.

Table 5.3C RATIO OF SHELTER NEED TO STANDARD OF NEED FOR FAMILY
SIZES OF THREE AND FOUR PERSONS, 1983-84[a]
(percent)

	Family size	
State and subdivision	Three persons	Four persons
Alabama	(30)	(30)
Alaska	(30)	(30)
Arizona	40	40
Arkansas	17	15
California	38	34
Colorado	27	27
Connecticut: Region A (high)	43	42
Connecticut: Region C (low)	33	30
Delaware	30	30
District of Columbia	(30)	(30)
Florida	34	29
Georgia	(30)	(30)
Hawaii	56	49
Idaho	26	23
Illinois	46	40
Indiana	32	27
Iowa	19	17
Kansas: Group I (low)	24	21
Kansas: Group II (high)	36	32
Kentucky	(30)	(30)
Louisiana	(30)	(30)
Maine	33	33
Maryland	37	37
Massachusetts	30	26
Michigan: Zone I (high)	25	25
Michigan: Zone II (low)	33	31
Minnesota	(30)	(30)
Mississippi	21	18
Missouri	(30)	(30)
Montana	50	49
Nebraska	30	25

Table 5.3C (continued)

State and subdivision	Family size	
	Three persons	Four persons
Nevada	(30)	(30)
New Hampshire: Regular housing (high)	36	32
New Hampshire: Subsidized housing (low)	25	42
New Jersey	(30)	(30)
New Mexico	34	34
New York: New York City (high)	55	51
New York: Erie County (low)	49	44
North Carolina	(30)	(30)
North Dakota	25	25
Ohio	(30)	(30)
Oklahoma	(30)	(30)
Oregon	37	36
Pennsylvania	(30)	(30)
Rhode Island	(30)	(30)
South Carolina	24	19
South Dakota	50	44
Tennessee	30	30
Texas	34	32
Utah	40	37
Vermont	38	33
Virginia: Group I (low)	46	43
Virginia: Group III (high)	53	50
Washington	55	52
West Virginia: Plan III (high)	21	19
West Virginia: Plan I (low)	0	0
Wisconsin	(30)	(30)
Wyoming	27	21

Source: State documents and telephone interviews with state welfare officials.

a. The numbers in parentheses are estimates for fully consolidated states.

Table 5.3D COMPARISON OF PAYMENT LEVEL FOR FAMILY SIZES OF THREE AND FOUR PERSONS, 1983-84 (dollars)

State and subdivision	Family size	
	Three persons	Four persons
Alabama	118	147
Alaska	719	800
Arizona	233	282
Arkansas	140	164
California	558	660
Colorado	346	420
Connecticut: Region A (high)	546	636
Connecticut: Region C (low)	460	534
Delaware	287	336
District of Columbia	327	399
Florida	240	284
Georgia	223	264
Hawaii	468	546
Idaho	304	344
Illinois	342	386
Indiana	256	316
Iowa	360	419
Kansas: Group I (low)	314	363
Kansas: Group II (high)	373	422
Kentucky	197	246
Louisiana: Region I (low)	174	217
Louisiana: Region II (high)	190	234
Maine	370	465
Maryland	313	376
Massachusetts	396	463
Michigan: Zone I (low)	420	516
Michigan: Zone II (high)	479	575
Minnesota	524	611
Mississippi	96	120
Missouri	265	310
Montana	332	425
Nebraska	350	420

Table 5.3D (continued)

	Family size	
State and subdivision	Three persons	Four persons
Nevada	234	280
New Hampshire: Regular housing (high)	389	442
New Hampshire: Subsidized housing (low)	367	418
New Jersey	381	443
New Mexico	258	313
New York: New York City (high)	444	528
New York: Erie County (low)	393	457
North Carolina	223	244
North Dakota	371	442
Ohio	276	343
Oklahoma: Schedule A (high)	282	349
Oklahoma: Schedule B (low)	234	301
Oregon	310	392
Pennsylvania	348	429
Rhode Island	424	484
South Carolina	187	229
South Dakota	329	371
Tennessee	138	168
Texas	167	201
Utah	367	428
Vermont	458	523
Virginia: Group I (low)	245	298
Virginia: Group III (high)	327	379
Washington	476	561
West Virginia: Plan III (high)	206	249
West Virginia: Plan I (low)	140	179
Wisconsin: Area I (high)	534	637
Wisconsin: Area II (low)	517	618
Wyoming	360	390

Source: State documents and telephone interviews with state welfare officials.

Table 5.3E COMPARISON OF SHELTER PAYMENTS FOR FAMILY SIZES OF
THREE AND FOUR PERSONS, 1983-84 (dollars)

State	Family size[a]		HUD Fair Market Rent[b]	
	Three persons	Four persons	High	Low
Alabama	(35)	(44)	356	254
Alaska	(216)	(240)	687	588
Arizona	93	112	445	328
Arkansas	24	24	331	228
California	211	222	577	335
Colorado	93	113	552	307
Connecticut: Region A (high)	237	265	491	340
Connecticut: Region C (low)	152	162	--	--
Delaware	86	101	421	361
District of Columbia	98	120	440	440
Florida	81	82	515	283
Georgia	(67)	(79)	397	261
Hawaii	240	265	552	507
Idaho	78	78	361	307
Illinois	158	155	572	247
Indiana	81	84	367	292
Iowa	67	72	382	287
Kansas: Group I	76	76	376	232
Kansas: Group II	135	135	--	--
Kentucky	(59)	(74)	386	236
Louisiana: Region I	(52)	(65)	375	228
Louisiana: Region II	(57)	(70)	--	--
Maine	123	155	450	339
Maryland	115	138	572	418
Massachusetts	119	119	533	364
Michigan: Zone I (low)	115	140	448	298
Michigan: Zone II (high)	170	195	--	--
Minnesota	(157)	(183)	451	280
Mississippi	20	22	387	279
Missouri	(80)	(93)	385	232
Montana	165	207	425	316
Nebraska	103	105	373	273

Table 5.3E (continued)

State	Family size[a] Three persons	Four persons	HUD Fair Market Rent[b] High	Low
Nevada	(70)	(84)	528	423
New Hampshire: Regular housing (high)	141	141	496	359
New Hampshire: Subsidized housing (low)	174	174	--	--
New Jersey	(114)	(133)	548	370
New Mexico	88	105	341	280
New York: New York City (high)	244	270	539	282
New York: Erie County (low)	193	199	--	--
North Carolina	(67)	(73)	377	246
North Dakota	93	114	491	310
Ohio	(83)	(103)	373	246
Oklahoma: Schedule A (high)	(85)	(105)	424	244
Oklahoma: Schedule B (low)	(70)	(90)	--	--
Oregon	116	140	408	302
Pennsylvania	(104)	(129)	402	237
Rhode Island	(127)	(145)	420	361
South Carolina	44	44	377	279
South Dakota	163	163	364	285
Tennessee	42	51	391	253
Texas	56	64	434	244
Utah	146	157	413	274
Vermont	173	173	478	351
Virginia: Group I (low)	112	127	415	266
Virginia: Group III (high)	173	189	--	--
Washington	260	292	461	302
West Virginia: Plan III (high)	43	47	451	387
West Virginia: Plan I (low)	0	0	--	--
Wisconsin: Area I (high)	160	191	451	273
Wisconsin: Area II (low)	155	185	--	--
Wyoming	95	80	478	307

Source: State documents and telephone interviews with state welfare officials.

a.   The numbers in parentheses are estimates for fully consolidated states.
b.   U.S. Department of Housing and Urban Development, rents for two-bedroom units.

Table 5.4   FEDERAL SHARE OF AFDC, BY STATE, 1983-84

State	Percentage	State	Percentage
Alabama	72.14	Montana	64.41
Alaska	50.00	Nebraska	57.13
Arizona	61.21	Nevada	50.00
Arkansas	73.65	New Hampshire	59.45
California	50.00	New Jersey	50.00
Colorado	50.00	New Mexico	69.39
Connecticut	50.00	New York	50.00
Delaware	50.00	North Carolina	69.54
District of		North Dakota	61.32
Columbia	50.00	Ohio	55.44
Florida	58.14	Oklahoma	58.47
Georgia	67.43	Oregon	57.12
Hawaii	50.00	Pennsylvania	56.04
Idaho	67.28	Puerto Rico	75.00
Illinois	50.00	Rhode Island	58.17
Indiana	59.93	South Carolina	73.51
Iowa	55.24	South Dakota	68.31
Kansas	50.67	Tennessee	70.66
Kentucky	70.72	Texas	54.37
Louisiana	64.65	Utah	70.84
Maine	70.63	Vermont	59.37
Maryland	50.00	Virginia	56.53
Massachusetts	50.13	Washington	50.00
Michigan	50.70	West Virginia	70.57
Minnesota	52.67	Wisconsin	56.87
Mississippi	77.63	Wyoming	50.00
Missouri	61.40		

Source: U.S. Congress, Background Material and Data on Programs within the Jurisdiction of the Committee on Ways and Means, 92 Cong., 1 sess., Committee Print WMCP 99-2. Washington, D.C., February 1985, pp. 356-57.

Table 5.5   HOUSEHOLD CHARACTERISTICS OF ELIGIBLE RECIPIENTS OF
AFDC, ALL STATES, 1984[a]

Household characteristics	Eligible states
Eligible children	All states
One needy parent or caretaker of child	All states except Mississippi
Second parent if one parent is incapacitated or principal earner is unemployed	All states except Alaska, Mississippi, and West Virginia
Unemployed principal earner who is the parent of at least one child[b]	California, Colorado, Connecticut, Delaware, District of Columbia, Hawaii, Illinois, Iowa, Kansas, Maryland, Massachusetts, Michigan, Minnesota, Missouri, Nebraska, New Jersey, New York, Ohio, Pennsylvania, Rhode Island, Vermont, Washington, West Virginia, and Wisconsin
"Essential" persons[c]	Arkansas, California, District of Columbia, Hawaii, Illinois, Iowa, Kansas, Louisiana, Maryland, Massachusetts, Minnesota, Missouri, New Jersey, New York, North Carolina, Oregon, Pennsylvania, Puerto Rico, Utah, Vermont, Virginia, Washington, and Wisconsin

Source: Research Tables from the Characteristics of State Plans for AFDC, U.S. Department of Health and Human Services. Washington, D.C., 1984.

a. All forty-eight states plus the District of Columbia, Alaska, Hawaii, and Puerto Rico.
b. For states with AFDC-UP (unemployed persons).
c. Any needy person living as a member of the family and performing an essential service. These persons are defined in various ways within the twenty-three states that include them in the grant.

Appendix DOCUMENTATION AND METHODOLOGY

The following provides the documentation for the procedures used to obtain a national distribution of family size for recipient families of AFDC and the method used to estimate distributions for each state. We start with two distributions of national data--the number of child recipients and the number of adult recipients.[1] These two distributions yield an estimate for the national distribution of family size of AFDC recipients. From state sources, we have obtained the average family size of recipients for each state. With this state-specific data, we adjust the national distribution and obtain an estimated distribution of family size for each state. A number of assumptions are made to obtain these estimated distributions.

The following table is the distribution of adult recipients in families enrolled in AFDC:

a	$f(a)$
0	0.088
1	0.799
2+	0.113

We call $f(a)$ the probability that an enrolled family has a adult recipients; and $g(c)$ is the probability that an enrolled family has c child recipients. The distribution for g is

c	$g(c)$
1	0.423
2	0.287
3	0.148
4	0.061
5	0.023
6+	0.015
zero (or unknown)	0.042

The probability of zero child recipients is set to zero, and the unknown portion of the distribution is assumed to be distributed in the same manner as the known cases:

Normalized

c	$g(c)$
1	0.4415
2	0.3000
3	0.1545
4	0.0637
5	0.0240
6+	0.0157

Two assumptions are required to derive the family size distribution. First, we assume that the distributions of g and f are independent. This means that the probability that an enrolled family has c recipient children is not related to the probability that the family has a adult recipients. The second assumption is that family size is the sum of the number of adult recipients and child recipients.

Let $h(a,c)$ be the joint distribution of adult and child recipients in a family. Since we assume that the distributions $g(c)$ and $f(a)$ are independent, we can compute the joint distribution $h(a,c)$ as the product of $g(c)$ and $f(a)$. We will use s as the sum of a and c. Thus

$$(s = a + c).$$

The next step is to specify all possible combinations of numbers of children and numbers of adults for each possible family size. We will not allow more than two adults per family, and we will explore family sizes of from one to six members only.

s	a	c
1	1	0
	0	1
2	0	2
	1	1
	2	0
3	0	3
	1	2
	2	1
4	0	4
	1	3
	2	2
5	0	5
	1	4
	2	3
6	0	6
	1	5
	2	4

We know that the probability that an enrolled family has two or more adult recipients is 0.113. We allow no more than two adults per family, based on the assumption that in actuality there are very few cases with more than two adult recipients. Using this assumption, we estimate that the probability that a family has exactly two adult recipients is approximately 0.113. In like manner, we assume the probability that a family has six or more child recipients is very close to the probability that a family has exactly six child recipients. These two assumptions can be expressed as

1. $f(a/a \geq 2) = f(2)$; *and*
2. $g(c/c \geq 6) = g(6)$.

Next, we compute the joint probabilities $h(a,c)$ to obtain the distri bution of s, family size:

1. $h(1) = h(1,0) + h(0,1) = f(1) \bullet g(0) + f(0) \bullet g(1)$
2. $h(2) = h(0,2) + h(1,1) + h(2,0) = f(0) \bullet g(2) + f(1) \bullet g(1) + f(2) \bullet g(0)$
   . . .
6. $h(6) = h(0,6) + h(1,5) + h(2,4)$.

The resulting distribution of family size is thus estimated to be

s	$h(s)$
1	0.0389
2	0.3792
3	0.3032
4	0.1630
5	0.0705
6	0.0278
	0.9826

Normalizing the distribution so that $\Sigma h(s) = 1$ produces:

Normalized

s	$h(s)$
1	0.0396
2	0.3859
3	0.3086
4	0.1659
5	0.0717
6	0.0283
	1.0000

This, then, becomes our estimated national distribution for family size for families enrolled in AFDC. We can obtain an average family size for the nation by computing the expected value for s:

$$2.9292 = \sum_{s=1}^{6} s \bullet h(s)$$

From the average monthly caseloads and monthly recipients data, we have computed average recipient family size for each state. These family sizes range from 2.25 in Colorado to 3.35 in Maine. Knowing the mean family size for each state enables us to modify the national distribution so that each state will have a slightly different distribution with the appropriate mean family size.

The method for adjusting the national distribution is demonstrated for a case in which the state mean family size is lower than the national mean. We use the case of Connecticut, with a mean family size of 2.7179. We start with $h(s)$, and we raise the probability of smaller size families while lowering the probability of large size families.

s	$K(s)$
1	$0.0396 + \Delta^1$
2	$0.3859 + \Delta^2$
3	$0.3086 - \Delta^3$
4	$0.1659 - \Delta^4$
5	$0.0717 - \Delta^5$
6	$0.0283 - \Delta^6$

We will call the modified distribution $K(s)$. The new distribution must necessarily sum to one, so we know that

$$\Delta_1 + \Delta_2 = \Delta_3 + \Delta_4 + \Delta_5 + \Delta_6.$$

We have only two equations: one that computes the mean, 2.7179, and the other that requires the sum of the final distribution to be equal to one. Thus we can allow only two unknowns. Each increment, Δ_i, can be expressed as a product of some α_i and $h(i)$.

s	$K(s)$
1	$0.0396 + 0.0396 \bullet \alpha_1$
2	$0.3859 + 0.3859 \bullet \alpha_2$
3	$0.3086 - 0.3086 \bullet \alpha_3$
4	$0.1659 - 0.1659 \bullet \alpha_4$
5	$0.0717 - 0.0717 \bullet \alpha_5$
6	$0.0283 - 0.0283 \bullet \alpha_6$

To reduce the number of unknowns to two, we now arbitrarily set $\alpha_1 = \alpha_2$, and $\alpha_3 = \alpha_4 = \alpha_5 = \alpha_6 = \beta_2$.
Let $\alpha_1 = \alpha_2 = \beta_1 = \alpha_3 = \alpha_4 = \alpha_5 = \alpha_6 = \beta_2$.

We know that

$$0.0396 \bullet \alpha_1 + 0.3859 \bullet \alpha_2 =$$
$$0.3086 \bullet \alpha_3 + 0.1659\, \alpha_4 + 0.0717\, \alpha_5 + 0.0283\, \alpha_6.$$

This simplifies to

$$(0.0389 + 0.3859)\beta_i = (0.3086 + 0.1659 + 0.0717 + 0.0283)\beta_2$$
$$0.4255\, \beta_1 = 0.5745\, \beta_2$$
$$\text{or}$$
$$\beta_1 = (1.35018) \bullet \beta_2.$$

Since we are trying to solve for the case where the expected value of s is 2.7179, our second equation is

$$E(s) = \sum_{s=1}^{6} s \bullet k(s)$$

Simplifying with the α_i, we obtain

s	$K(s)$	$s \bullet K(s)$
1	$0.0396 + 0.0396\, \beta_1$	$0.0396 + 0.0396\, \beta_1$
2	$0.3859 + 0.3859\, \beta_1$	$0.7718 + 0.7718\, \beta_1$
3	$0.3086 - 0.3086\, \beta_2$	$0.9258 - 0.9258\, \beta_2$
4	$0.1659 - 0.1659\, \beta_2$	$0.6636 - 0.6636\, \beta_2$
5	$0.0717 - 0.0717\, \beta_2$	$0.3585 - 0.3585\, \beta_2$
6	$0.0283 - 0.0283\, \beta_2$	$0.1698 - 0.1698\, \beta_2$

$$2.9291 + 0.8114 - 2.1177\, \beta_2 = 2.7179$$

$$0.2112 + 0.8114\, \beta_1 = 2.1177\, \beta_2.$$

Substituting $1.35018\, \beta_2$ for β_1, we obtain

$$0.2112 + 0.8114(1.35018)\, \beta_2 = 2.1177\, \beta_2$$
$$0.2112 + 1.0955\, \beta_2 = 2.1177\, \beta_2$$
$$0.2112 = 1.0222\, \beta_2$$
$$0.2066 = \beta_2.$$

Thus $\beta_1 = 0.2790$.

Applying this methodology to the state of Connecticut, for example, produces the following estimated distribution:

s	$K(s)$
1	0.0506
2	0.5946
3	0.2448
4	0.1316
5	0.0569
6	0.0225
	1.0000

and $\Sigma s \bullet k(s) = 2.718$.

Had we picked a state with a mean family size larger than the national average, we would have lowered the probabilities associated with families with one and two members, and we would have raised the probabilities associated with families with three through six members.

In general if we use

$$1 = 1.35018 \, \beta_2$$
$$2 = \frac{2.9291 - \mu_i}{1.0222}.$$

The formula to use in constructing the state-specific distribution involves <u>adding</u> $\beta_1 \bullet h(s)$ for $s = 1, 2$, and <u>subtracting</u> $\beta_2 \bullet h(s)$ for $s \geq 3$.

This applies whether the state mean is lower or higher than the national mean family size.

Note

1. <u>Background Material and Data on Programs within the Jurisdiction of the Committee on Ways and Means</u>, 99 Cong., 1 sess. (Washington, D.C.: U. S. Government Printing Office, February 1985), Committee Print WMCP 99-2, table 19, p. 368.

6

SUPPLEMENTAL SECURITY INCOME

BACKGROUND

The Supplemental Security Income (SSI) program[1] is a federally administered income assistance program authorized by Title XVI of the Social Security Act. Established in 1972 (Public Law 92-603) and begun in 1974, SSI provides cash payments on a monthly basis in accordance with uniform, nationwide eligibility standards to needy aged, blind, and disabled persons. The program consolidates old-age assistance (OA), aid to the blind (AB), and aid to the partially and totally disabled (APTD) and applies uniform eligibility and benefit standards.

Part of the motivation for creating SSI was to supplement regular Social Security benefits for low-income individuals.[2] Nonrecipients of Social Security were included in the SSI program if they met eligibility criteria. According to the Committee on Ways and Means, "Some people who because of age, disability or blindness are not able to support themselves receive relatively small social security benefits. Contributory social insurance, therefore, must be supplemented by an effective assistance program."[3]

Benefit standards for SSI are based on the poverty threshold. The program's goal is to keep needy aged, blind, or disabled individuals from falling below the poverty line. Benefits are indexed to the consumer price index by the same formula used for Social Security benefits. In 1985 the federal SSI benefit standard was $325 a month for an individual recipient, $488 for a couple, and $163 for an "essential" person.

157

Currently SSI is administered in the fifty states, the District of Columbia, and the Northern Mariana Islands. Guam, Puerto Rico, and the Virgin Islands continue to administer OA, AB, and APTD.

SSI and Shelter Assistance. The SSI law provides that if an applicant or recipient is living in another person's household and receives support and maintenance in-kind from such a person, the value of this in-kind assistance is presumed to equal one-third of the federal SSI benefit standard. Thus, the implicit shelter allowance equals roughly 33 percent of the federal SSI benefit standard. (In 1984, roughly 5.6 percent of SSI recipients had their payments reduced under this one-third rule.)

If an individual owns or rents the living quarters or contributes a pro rata share to the household expenses, the one-third deduction does not apply. Applicants and recipients may challenge the one-third deduction. If it is determined that the value of such in-kind assistance is less than the one-third deduction, SSI benefits are recalculated but can never exceed the amounts set as the federal SSI benefit standard.

Income Disregards. Under SSI, $20.00 of monthly income from virtually any source (such as Social Security benefits, but not needs-tested income such as veterans' benefits) is disregarded. In addition, the first $65.00 of monthly earned income plus one-half of remaining earnings are disregarded. The value of in-kind assistance is counted as income unless such in-kind assistance is specifically disregarded by statute. General in-kind assistance provided by or under the auspices of a federally assisted program or by a state or local government (for example, nutrition, food stamps, housing or social services), will not be counted as income. The income of an ineligible spouse who lives with an adult SSI applicant or recipient and the parents of a disabled or blind child under eighteen are considered in determining eligibility and benefit standards.

In legislation enacted in April 1983, in-kind support and maintenance provided by a private, nonprofit organization to aged, blind, or disabled individuals must be disregarded under the SSI program if the state determines the assistance is provided on the basis of need. Another exclusion from countable income is certain types of assistance to meet home energy needs.

Eligibility for SSI ends when countable income equals the federal SSI benefit standard plus the amount of any state supplementation.

Resources. SSI eligibility is restricted to qualified persons who have counted assets of less than $1,600.00 or less than $2,400.00 in the case of a couple. The Deficit Reduction Act of 1984 (Public Law 98-369) will increase countable asset limitations by $100.00 per year for an individual and $150.00 per year for a couple. The limit will be $2,000.00 per year for an individual and $3,000.00 per year for a couple in 1989 and thereafter.

An individual's home is not included when determining assets.

State Supplementation of SSI. Although the federal benefit payment under SSI is uniform across all states, the states have full discretion to supplement these payments for all, or particular subgroups of, SSI eligibles. If a state provides a supplement, it is required by federal law to maintain income levels of former public assistance recipients who are transferred to the federal SSI program. States also have the option to supplement the federal SSI benefit standard for other SSI recipients. As of 1984, all but eight states and jurisdictions provided some form of optional state supplementation;[4] only twenty-eight states, however, do not earmark these supplements for special residential facilities for the disabled.

Approximately 43 percent of SSI recipients receive a state supplement. The amount ranges from $1.70 (Oregon) to $261.00 (Alaska) for an individual living independently. Of the twenty-eight states that provide general supplements to the federal SSI benefit, fifteen states provide the same amount of supplementation for those whose federal SSI benefit standard is determined on the basis of the one-third reduction. Seven states provide a higher state supplementation for such recipients, and six states provide less.[5]

SUMMARY STATISTICS ON SHELTER ASSISTANCE UNDER SSI, BY STATE

Table 6.1 provides information on the size of each state's SSI recipient population, the amount of the state's supplementary payment (excluding those for special housing for the disabled), the implicit shelter subsidy embedded in the SSI benefit payment, and the relation between the SSI shelter subsidy and the rent required for a minimally adequate unit.

The SSI shelter subsidy was estimated in two ways. In the first approach (labeled method I in the table), this benefit is set at one-third of the total payment made to a qualified person living independently.[6] This approach reflects the valuation of living in another person's household at two-thirds the cost of living independently, as described earlier. The second approach (method II) applies the one-third factor to the federal portion of the payment but applies each state's specific valuation of joint versus independent living to the state portion. (See Part 1 for details.)

The rent level used to evaluate the adequacy of the SSI shelter payment is HUD's Fair Market Rent (FMR) for an efficiency unit in the Section 8 existing housing program. The FMR represents the minimum amount required for a unit that is decent, safe, and sanitary in each housing market area. Since each state contains several market areas, the minimum FMR was used for the adequacy calculation. In contrast, the SSI shelter amount used in the numerator of the ratio is the maximum payment an individual can receive in each state. Thus, the resulting ratios shown in the last two columns of the table (method I, FMR, and method II, FMR) set an upper bound on the estimated adequacy of SSI shelter assistance.

Table 6.2 provides information, by state, on monthly recipients, total SSI expenditures, and SSI shelter expenditures. The latter were estimated using the 33 percent rule. Here, too, the estimates set an upper bound both because the one-third valuation covers more than just shelter and because the total SSI expenditure estimates include state special housing SSI funding. The latter could not be extracted from available data.[7]

Notes

1. This section relies heavily on Background Material and Data on Programs within the Jurisdiction of the Committee on Ways and Means, 99 Cong., 1 sess., Committee Print WMCP 99-2. Washington, D.C. February 1985.
2. In June 1984, 71 percent of the aged, 38 percent of the blind, and 36 percent of the disabled receiving SSI were also Social Security recipients.
3. Social Security Amendments of 1971, U.S. House of Representatives, Committee on Ways and Means, Report 92-231, 92 Cong., 1 sess. Washington, D.C (26 May 1971).
4. Arkansas, Georgia, Kansas, Mississippi, Northern Mariana Islands, Tennessee, Texas, and West Virginia.
5. A significant share of state SSI supplement programs is for the special housing needs of such populations as the chronically mentally ill and the physically disabled. In 1985, forty-four states and jurisdictions had state supplements that cover the additional cost of providing housing in a protective, supervised, or group living arrangement. The amount of state supplementation varied by state. These special supplements were excluded from the present analysis.
6. This method should result in an upper-bound value since the one-third estimate includes more than just shelter.
7. This amount is not expected to dramatically overstate SSI expenditures.

Table 6.1 SUMMARY STATISTICS ON SHELTER ASSISTANCE UNDER SSI, BY STATE, 1984-85 DATA

Region and state	Number of persons with SSI	Assistance for persons living independently (dollars)				Assistance for persons living in another's household (dollars)			
		Maximum federal and state SSI benefit level		Amount of state supplement		Maximum federal and state SSI benefit level		Amount of state supplement	
		Individual	Couple	Individual	Couple	Individual	Couple	Individual	Couple
Northeast									
Connecticut	23,943	465.70	574.20	140.70	86.20	357.37	411.54	140.70	86.20
Maine	20,684	335.00	503.00	10.00	15.00	224.67	337.34	8.00	12.00
Massachusetts	108,378	453.82	689.72	128.82	201.72	321.03	541.14	104.36	215.80
New Hampshire	5,308	339.00	489.00	14.00	1.00	243.67	346.34	27.00	21.00
New Jersey	85,078	356.25	513.36	31.25	25.36	260.98	418.43	44.31	93.06
New York	336,463	385.91	564.03	60.91	76.03	224.91	352.37	8.24	27.03
Pennsylvania	154,026	357.40	536.70	32.40	48.70	249.07	374.04	32.40	48.70
Rhode Island	14,482	378.80	589.74	53.80	101.74	279.65	440.57	62.98	115.23
Vermont	8,743	378.00	584.50	53.00	96.50	251.97	370.14	35.30	44.80
Total weighted average	757,105	387.07	569.62	62.07	81.62	253.31	394.53	36.64	69.19

Table 6.1 (continued)

| Region and state | Number of persons with SSI | Assistance for persons living independently (dollars) | | | | Assistance for persons living in another's household (dollars) | | | |
| | | Maximum federal and state SSI benefit level | | Amount of state supplement | | Maximum federal and state SSI benefit level | | Amount of state supplement | |
		Individual	Couple	Individual	Couple	Individual	Couple	Individual	Couple
North Central									
Illinois	119,761	360.23	521.70	35.23	33.70	251.90	359.04	35.23	33.70
Indiana	40,532	325.00	488.00	0.00	0.00	216.67	325.34	0.00	0.00
Iowa	25,530	347.00	532.00	22.00	44.00	238.67	369.34	22.00	44.00
Kansas	19,549	325.00	488.00	0.00	0.00	216.67	325.34	0.00	0.00
Michigan	110,542	351.70	528.00	26.70	40.00	235.27	353.17	18.60	27.83
Minnesota	29,852	360.00	554.00	35.00	66.00	276.00	484.00	59.33	158.66
Missouri	77,074	325.00	488.00	35.00	0.00	216.67	325.34	0.00	0.00
Nebraska	13,001	386.00	580.00	68.50	99.50	285.17	424.84	68.50	99.50
North Dakota	5,838	325.00	488.00	0.00	0.00	216.67	325.34	0.00	0.00
Ohio	115,324	325.00	488.00	0.00	0.00	216.67	325.34	0.00	0.00
South Dakota	7,663	340.00	503.00	15.00	15.00	231.67	340.34	15.00	15.00
Wisconsin	62,610	424.70	649.00	99.70	161.00	316.37	486.34	99.70	161.00
Total weighted average	627,276	350.29	524.57	25.55	36.73	241.95	364.34	25.28	39.00

Table 6.1 (continued)

Region and state	Number of persons with SSI	Assistance for persons living independently (dollars)				Assistance for persons living in another's household (dollars)			
		Maximum federal and state SSI benefit level		Amount of state supplement		Maximum federal and state SSI benefit level		Amount of state supplement	
		Individual	Couple	Individual	Couple	Individual	Couple	Individual	Couple
South									
Alabama	127,849	325.00	488.00	0.00	0.00	216.67	325.34	0.00	0.00
Arkansas	71,503	325.00	488.00	0.00	0.00	216.67	325.34	0.00	0.00
Delaware	6,893	325.00	488.00	0.00	0.00	216.67	325.34	0.00	0.00
District of Columbia	14,758	340.00	518.00	15.00	30.00	231.67	355.34	15.00	30.00
Florida	170,904	325.00	488.00	0.00	0.00	216.67	324.34	0.00	0.00
Georgia	147,945	325.00	488.00	0.00	0.00	216.67	324.34	0.00	0.00
Kentucky	91,685	325.00	488.00	0.00	0.00	216.67	325.34	0.00	0.00
Louisiana	123,093	325.00	488.00	0.00	0.00	216.67	325.34	0.00	0.00
Maryland	47,197	325.00	488.00	0.00	0.00	216.67	325.34	0.00	0.00
Mississippi	109,063	325.00	488.00	0.00	0.00	216.67	325.34	0.00	0.00
North Carolina	131,937	385.00	608.00	60.00	120.00	276.67	445.34	60.00	120.00
Oklahoma	59,081	325.00	488.00	0.00	0.00	216.67	325.34	0.00	0.00
South Carolina	81,071	325.00	488.00	0.00	0.00	216.67	325.34	0.00	0.00
Tennessee	124,149	325.00	488.00	0.00	0.00	216.67	325.34	0.00	0.00
Texas	244,278	325.00	488.00	0.00	0.00	216.67	325.34	0.00	0.00
Virginia	79,320	325.00	488.00	0.00	0.00	216.67	325.34	0.00	0.00
West Virginia	39,571	325.00	488.00	0.00	0.00	216.67	325.34	0.00	0.00
Total weighted average	1,670,297	327.25	492.51	2.25	4.51	218.92	329.66	2.25	4.51

Table 6.1 (continued)

Region and state	Number of persons with SSI	Assistance for persons living independently (dollars)				Assistance for persons living in another's household (dollars)			
		Maximum federal and state SSI benefit level		Amount of state supplement		Maximum federal and state SSI benefit level		Amount of state supplement	
		Individual	Couple	Individual	Couple	Individual	Couple	Individual	Couple
West									
Alaska	3,015	586.00	859.00	261.00	371.00	482.00	707.00	265.33	381.66
Arizona	29,236	325.00	488.00	0.00	0.00	216.67	325.34	0.00	0.00
California	653,383	504.00	936.00	179.00	448.00	395.67	773.34	179.00	448.00
Colorado	28,366	383.00	766.00	58.00	278.00	274.67	603.34	58.00	278.00
Hawaii	9,980	329.90	496.80	4.90	8.80	221.57	334.14	4.90	8.80
Idaho	7,542	383.00	514.00	58.50	26.00	294.67	371.34	78.00	46.00
Montana	6,678	325.00	488.00	0.00	0.00	216.67	325.34	0.00	0.00
Nevada	6,899	361.40	562.46	36.40	74.46	240.94	374.97	24.27	49.63
New Mexico	24,600	325.00	488.00	0.00	0.00	216.67	325.34	0.00	0.00
Oregon	23,123	326.70	488.00	1.70	0.00	218.37	325.34	1.70	0.00
Utah	7,835	335.00	508.00	10.00	20.00	226.67	345.34	10.00	20.00
Washington	43,730	363.30	525.40	38.30	37.40	229.35	341.91	12.68	16.57
Wyoming	1,796	345.00	528.00	20.00	40.00	236.67	365.34	20.00	40.00
Total weighted average	846,183	469.12	847.71	144.12	359.71	359.56	683.99	142.89	358.65
National total weighted average	3,900,861	373.36	589.68	48.38	101.71	259.81	424.69	43.14	99.43

Table 6.1 (continued)

	Shelter payments: Methods I and II						
Region and state	33 percent (living independently)		33 percent (federal, living independently) plus x percent (state supplement)		HUD Fair Market Rent[a]	Method I Fair Market Rent (percent)	Method II Fair Market Rent (percent)
	Individual	Couple	Individual	Couple			
Northeast							
Connecticut	155.23	191.40	200[b]	200[b]	239	64.95	83.68
Maine	111.67	167.67	110	166	248	45.03	44.35
Massachusetts	151.27	229.91	133	234[c]	261	57.96	50.96
New Hampshire	113.00	163.00	117[c]	170[c]	269	42.01	43.49
New Jersey	118.75	171.12	123[c]	194[c]	265	44.81	46.42
New York	128.64	188.01	161	212	191	67.35	84.29
Pennsylvania	119.13	178.90	119	179	155	76.86	76.86
Rhode Island	126.27	196.58	133[d]	201[d]	267	47.29	49.81
Vermont	126.00	194.83	126	215	254	49.61	49.61
Total weighted average	129.02	189.87	144	206	208	63.96	71.30

Table 6.1 (continued)

Region and state	Shelter payments: Methods I and II				HUD Fair Market Rent[a]	Method I Fair Market Rent (percent)	Method II Fair Market Rent (percent)
	33 percent (living independently)		33 percent (federal, living independently) plus x percent (state supplement)				
	Individual	Couple	Individual	Couple			
North Central							
Illinois	120.08	173.90	120	174	169	71.05	71.01
Indiana	108.33	162.67	108	163	205	52.85	52.85
Iowa	115.67	177.33	115	178	201	57.55	57.21
Kansas	108.33	162.67	108	163	159	68.13	68.13
Michigan	117.23	176.00	116	175	208	56.36	55.77
Minnesota	120.00	184.67	120	185	195	61.54	61.54
Missouri	108.33	162.67	108[b]	163[b]	159	68.13	68.13
Nebraska	128.67	193.33	140[b]	175[b]	188	68.44	74.47
North Dakota	108.33	162.67	108	163	207	52.33	52.33
Ohio	108.33	162.67	108	163	155	69.89	69.89
South Dakota	113.33	167.67	113	168	199	56.95	56.78
Wisconsin	141.57	216.33	141[e]	216[e]	188	75.30	75.00
Total weighted average	116.80	174.86	117	174	180	65.65	65.59

Table 6.1 (continued)

Region and state	Shelter payments: Methods I and II				HUD Fair Market Rent[a]	Method I Fair Market Rent (percent)	Method II Fair Market Rent (percent)
	33 percent (living independently)		33 percent (federal, living independently) plus x percent (state supplement)				
	Individual	Couple	Individual	Couple			
South							
Alabama	108.33	162.67	108	163	176	61.55	61.55
Arkansas	108.33	162.67	108	163	156	69.44	69.44
Delaware	108.33	162.67	108	163	244	44.40	44.40
District of Columbia	113.33	172.67	113	173	319	35.53	35.42
Florida	108.33	162.67	108	163	198	54.71	54.71
Georgia	108.33	162.67	108	163	184	58.88	58.88
Kentucky	108.33	162.67	108	163	169	64.10	64.10
Louisiana	108.33	162.67	108	163	156	69.44	69.44
Maryland	108.33	162.67	108	163	244	44.40	44.40
Mississippi	108.33	162.67	108	163	193	56.13	56.13
North Carolina	108.33	162.67	108	163	170	63.73	63.73
Oklahoma	128.33	202.67	128	203	167	76.85	76.65
South Carolina	108.33	162.67	108	163	194	55.84	55.84
Tennessee	108.33	162.67	108	163	174	62.26	62.26
Texas	108.33	162.67	108	163	167	64.87	64.87
Virginia	108.33	162.67	108	163	183	59.20	59.20
West Virginia	108.33	162.67	108	163	201	53.90	53.90
Total weighted average	109.08	164.17	109	164	180	61.22	61.21

Table 6.1 (continued)

Region and state	Shelter payments: Methods I and II						
	33 percent (living independently)		33 percent (federal, living independently) plus x percent (state supplement)		HUD Fair Market Rent[a]	Method I Fair Market Rent (percent)	Method II Fair Market Rent (percent)
	Individual	Couple	Individual	Couple			
West							
Alaska	195.33	286.33	196[c]	289[c]	403	48.47	48.64
Arizona	108.33	162.67	108	163	233	46.49	46.35
California	168.00	312.00	167	311	237	70.89	70.46
Colorado	127.67	255.33	127	255	214	59.66	55.14
Hawaii	109.97	165.60	110	166	370	29.72	29.73
Idaho	127.67	171.33	118[b]	118[b]	214	59.66	114.80
Montana	108.33	162.67	108	163	225	48.15	48.15
Nevada	120.47	187.49	120	188	297	40.56	40.40
New Mexico	108.33	162.67	108	163	197	54.99	54.99
Oregon	108.90	162.67	109	163	200	54.45	54.50
Utah	111.67	169.33	111	170	192	58.16	57.81
Washington	121.10	175.13	134	184	236	51.31	56.78
Wyoming	115.00	176.00	115	176	214	53.74	53.74
Total weighted average	156.37	282.57	157	283	236	66.50	66.40
National total weighted average	124.45	196.56	128	200	198	63.61	65.00

Table 6.1 (continued)

Source: State documents, telephone interviews with state officials, and The SSI Program for the Aged, Blind, and Disabled. Social Security Administration, Washington, D.C. 1985.(6).

Note: Methods **I** and **II** are described in the text.

a. Zero bedroom minimum.
b. Explicit shelter maximum under **SSI** (both federal and state).
c. States that increase their supplement payment for joint households to reflect costs of caretaking. Shelter payment calculated at 33 percent of the supplement for joint living arrangement.
d. Rhode Island increases its supplement payments for joint households to reflect increased rental costs and costs of caretaking. State welfare officials estimate the shelter component at 40 percent of the payment.
e. Wisconsin officials estimate shelter component at 45 percent of supplement payment for independent living.

Table 6.2 AGGREGATE INFORMATION ON SSI: RECIPIENTS
           AND EXPENDITURES, 1984-85

Region and state	Recipients per month	SSI expenditures (dollars)	Shelter expenditures (dollars)
Northeast			
Connecticut	23,943	90,704,000	30,231,643
Maine	20,684	39,275,000	13,090,358
Massachusetts	108,378	276,331,000	92,101,122
New Hampshire	5,308	20,531,000	6,842,982
New Jersey	85,078	235,438,000	78,471,485
New York	336,463	982,478,000	327,459,917
Pennsylvania	154,026	403,593,000	134,517,547
Rhode Island	14,482	35,162,000	11,719,495
Vermont	8,743	21,781,000	7,259,607
Total Northeast	757,105	2,105,293,000	701,694,157
North Central			
Illinois	119,761	329,076,000	109,681,031
Indiana	40,532	92,139,000	30,709,929
Iowa	25,530	50,455,000	16,816,652
Kansas	19,549	40,248,000	13,414,658
Michigan	110,542	308,957,000	102,975,368
Minnesota	29,852	68,677,000	22,890,044
Missouri	77,074	175,621,000	58,534,479
Nebraska	13,001	32,003,000	10,666,600
North Dakota	5,838	12,859,000	4,285,905
Ohio	115,324	283,768,000	94,579,874
South Dakota	7,663	15,625,000	5,207,813
Wisconsin	62,610	159,742,000	53,242,009
Total North Central	627,276	1,569,170,000	523,004,361
South			
Alabama	127,849	275,422,000	91,798,153
Arkansas	71,503	136,068,000	45,351,464
District of Columbia	14,758	41,935,000	13,976,936
Delaware	6,893	15,637,000	5,211,812
Florida	170,904	422,507,000	140,821,583
Georgia	147,945	310,531,000	103,499,982
Kentucky	91,685	224,108,000	74,695,196

Table 6.2 (continued)

Region and state	Recipients per month	SSI expenditures (dollars)	Shelter expenditures (dollars)
South (continued)			
Louisiana	123,093	276,001,000	91,991,133
Maryland	47,197	119,782,000	39,923,341
Mississippi	109,063	230,384,000	76,786,987
North Carolina	131,937	315,180,000	105,049,494
Oklahoma	59,081	151,108,000	50,364,296
South Carolina	81,071	174,868,000	58,283,504
Tennessee	124,149	268,022,000	89,331,733
Texas	244,278	483,945,000	161,298,869
Virginia	79,320	181,721,000	60,567,609
West Virginia	39,571	99,015,000	33,001,700
Total South	1,670,290	3,726,234,000	1,241,953,792
West			
Alaska	3,015	20,177,000	6,724,994
Arizona	29,236	78,323,000	26,105,056
California	653,383	2,238,685,000	746,153,711
Colorado	28,366	110,251,000	36,746,658
Hawaii	9,980	27,533,000	9,176,749
Idaho	7,542	20,280,000	6,759,324
Montana	6,678	15,164,000	5,054,161
Nevada	6,899	16,575,000	5,524,448
New Mexico	24,600	56,578,000	18,857,447
Oregon	23,123	67,760,000	22,584,408
Utah	7,835	18,178,000	6,058,727
Washington	43,730	116,048,000	38,678,798
Wyoming	1,796	3,975,000	1,324,868
Total West	846,183	2,789,527,000	929,749,349
National Total	3,900,861	10,190,224,000	3,396,401,659

Source: State documents, telephone interviews with state officials, and The SSI Program for the Aged, Blind, and Disabled. Social Security Administration, Washington, D.C., 1985 (6).

7

GENERAL ASSISTANCE

BACKGROUND

General Assistance (GA) is the generic title for state and local welfare programs that provide income and service assistance to needy persons who do not qualify for federal-state categorical assistance programs. These individuals usually meet financial eligibility criteria for categorical assistance but not other demographic or disability requirements.

As shown in table 7.1, in fiscal 1984, GA programs existed in thirty-eight states. (Two states, Alabama and West Virginia, had essentially no assistance available for GA populations. In another ten states--Alaska, Arkansas, Idaho, Indiana, Mississippi, North Carolina, Oklahoma, South Carolina, Tennessee, and Vermont--only short-term or one-time Emergency Assistance was available.)

In most cases, eligible recipients represent a fairly general cross-section of needy populations who fall through the AFDC and SSI net. A recent report on the characteristics of general relief recipients in Los Angeles provides a succinct profile of the typical GA recipient: a forty-three year-old, never married, black male, who is not a veteran and is unemployable yet not able to meet SSI disability criteria.[1] Some programs, particularly in the South, however, are more limited, restricting coverage only to disabled individuals awaiting eligibility determinations for, or coverage by, SSI.

Table 7.1 also indicates that GA program funding is provided by twenty-six states, roughly three-quarters of all states in which GA programs exist. The remaining states, counties, or localities either contribute toward the funding pool or assume sole responsibility for funding. In some of these states (for example, Virginia and North Dakota) the state reimburses the locality for some predetermined percentage of local assistance and administrative expenses.

In eighteen states, many fundamentals of GA programs, such as recipient eligibility rules, the amount of the GA payment, and the length of time a recipient can receive GA, are determined by counties or localities. Although these jurisdictions are given discretion in designing and administering GA programs, many states (such as Maine, Illinois, and Michigan) set minimum standards to which localities must conform. More generally, many state constitutions include language that requires the provision of assistance to all residents to enable them to reach minimal subsistence. The interpretation of these provisions by both state and local welfare administrators has resulted in class-action lawsuits in a number of states on behalf of welfare recipients.

Table 7.2 summarizes several additional characteristics of GA programs across the nation. Approximately the same number of states contain GA programs with consolidated payments as states with explicit maximum grants for particular purchases, such as food or shelter. The trend toward consolidation, however, is clear: several states, including Minnesota and Illinois, moved to consolidated payments in the early 1980s and a number of other states, such as Ohio, are seriously considering consolidation.

In the majority of states the GA payments are based on a standard of need, often the same one developed for AFDC. Yet the benefits of this systematic approach to establishing payment levels are greatly diluted in most cases because either the underlying standards are not updated to reflect changes in the cost of living or the payment levels are set at only a fraction of the needs standards.

SUMMARY STATISTICS ON SHELTER ASSISTANCE UNDER GENERAL ASSISTANCE, BY STATE

The importance of counties and localities in determining the nature of GA programs across the nation results in a multiplicity of programs that often defy comparison. We, therefore, made a number of simplifying assumptions to provide a state-by-state, regional, and national picture of this third component of the nation's welfare system. In the twenty states with statewide GA programs, we were able to develop state-level GA characteristics through interviews with state officials and reviews of state budget and research documents. In the remaining eighteen states in which GA programs are inherently local programs, we took one of two approaches: in most cases, we collected information on the one or two counties that accounted for the largest proportion of GA expenditures in the state and inflated these estimates to form state aggregates.   For example, Clark and Washoe Counties comprise roughly 90 percent of all GA expenditures in Nevada; Harris County (Houston) represents roughly 75 percent of Texas GA expenditures, and Dade County (Miami) covers about 90 percent of GA expenditures in Florida.   In the remaining states, we relied on various sources (for example, interviews with state officials, county welfare administrators, surveys of the Association of County Welfare Directors, and the like) to develop a picture of state GA characteristics.   Because the states with the largest GA expenditures also tend to be the ones with the most detailed documentation on their programs, errors in our estimates are probably small and are unlikely to affect the overall conclusions substantially.

Table 7.3 summarizes the aggregate characteristics of GA.   We estimate that in fiscal 1984, a total of $2.3 billion was spent in thirty-eight states on GA programs; roughly 60 percent of these expenditures, or $1.4 billion, was devoted to defraying recipient shelter costs. Variations in program size are staggering.   Regionally, for example, the Northeast has more than nine times as many recipients as the South and spends more than fourteen times as much for both total GA grants and for shelter assistance.   The Northeast, in fact, accounts for roughly 50 percent of the nation's GA expenditures; the South accounts for about 3.2 percent.[2]

Table 7.4 provides information on the actual payments received by GA recipients and the adequacy of the shelter portion of the payment relative to the Fair Market Rent.   The marked variation in GA shelter payments and in the proportion of total GA payments that these shelter amounts represent are evident.   There is considerable dispersion around the national average GA shelter payment of $129.   Payments across the country range from a low of $36 in Arizona to a high of $311 in Maine.   Even if these two states were eliminated as outliers, however, GA shelter payments would continue to present a wide range, from less than $100 to $200 or more.

The dispersion in shelter payments is closely related to the dispersion in total GA payments per recipient.   Nevada is a clear exception to this rule, however; although its total GA payment is among the 10 highest in the nation at $228 per month, its shelter payment is only 25 percent of this amount, or $57.   Since Nevada's payment standard is explicit, this means that $57 is the maximum grant a GA recipient can receive to defray housing expenses, unless a special exception is granted.

Regionally, the absolute level of shelter payments is lowest in the South and highest in the Northeast and West.   Because of sharp variations in the number of recipients per state and in the generosity of the shelter payments, the West, for example, can encompass several small states with among the lowest payments in the nation and still retain a high average GA shelter payment.

In contrast to the generally close relationship between total GA payments and the amount that is directed toward shelter costs, GA shelter payments bear little resemblance to the minimum Fair Market Rent in each state. Here, too, the average shelter payment to FMR ratio for the nation hides sizable disparities in this ratio across the country. Only in New York, North Dakota, and Iowa are shelter payments for a single individual and FMRs for efficiency units roughly equal. In another six states, these GA payments provide at least three-quarters of the estimated cost of minimally standard housing.[3] But in the majority of states, this ratio is much lower, and reaches less than 30 percent in six states.[4]

Another variation of GA programs both within and across states is the disparity in payments by family size. As shown in table 7.5, variations in shelter payments for one person families even within a single region range from $36 in Arizona to $189 in Washington.

A final characteristic of the nation's GA programs, and one that distinguishes it from both AFDC and SSI, is that in five states, at least some programs were reported to conduct housing inspections to ensure the adequacy of shelter for GA recipients. These states are Connecticut, Florida, New York, Rhode Island and Wisconsin, with the most extensive operations in Westchester County, New York; Waterford, Connecticut; and Madison, Wisconsin. Varying approaches are taken in these states. In some cases, the GA caseworker inspects the dwelling only if there is compelling evidence that the recipient is occupying a dangerously inadequate unit, while in others, virtually all units are inspected. The issue of housing inspections has not been ignored in most of the other states, however. As one state official reported, in response to our specific survey question regarding the use of housing inspections, although housing inspections had been seriously considered, it was feared that the main result would be more homelessness.

Notes

1. General Relief Recipient Characteristics Study. County Department of Public Social Services. Los Angeles, California. December 1982, p. 1.
2. See Part 1, chapter 2 for further discussion of differences in welfare program size that relate to the size of the total poverty population in each state.
3. Connecticut, Georgia, Michigan, Minnesota, Oregon, and Washington.
4. Arizona, Delaware, Maryland, Nevada, South Dakota, and Wyoming.

Table 7.1 OVERVIEW OF GENERAL ASSISTANCE AND EMERGENCY ASSISTANCE PROGRAMS, BY STATE, 1984-85

Region and state	Administrative control	Funding source	Program type	Duration of assistance available	Main recipients
Northeast					
Connecticut	Local	State	General Assistance	Long-term	Needy
Maine	Local	State	General Assistance	Long-term	Needy
Massachusetts	State	State	General Assistance	Long-term	Needy
New Hampshire	Local	Local	General Assistance	Temporary	Needy
New Jersey	State	State	General Assistance	Long-term	Needy
New York	State	State	General Assistance	Long-term	Needy
Pennsylvania	State	State	General Assistance	Long-term	Needy
Rhode Island	Local	State	General Assistance	Long-term	Needy
Vermont	State	State	Emergency Assistance	Temporary	NA
North Central					
Illinois	State	State	General Assistance	Long-term	Needy
Indiana	Local	Local	Emergency Assistance	Temporary	NA
Iowa	County	County	General Assistance	One-time	Needy
Kansas	State	State	General Assistance	Long-term	Needy
Michigan	State	State	General Assistance	Long-term	Needy
Minnesota	State	State	General Assistance	Long-term	Needy
Missouri	State	State	General Assistance	Long-term	Disabled SSI applicants
Nebraska	State, county	County	General Assistance	Long-term	Needy
North Dakota	County	State, county	General Assistance	One-time	NA
Ohio	State	State	General Assistance	Long-term	Needy
South Dakota	County	County	General Assistance	One-time	NA
Wisconsin	County, local	County, local	General Assistance	Long-term	Needy

Table 7.1 (continued)

Region and state	Administrative control	Funding source	Program type	Duration of assistance available	Main recipients
South					
Arkansas	State	State	Emergency Assistance	One-time	NA
District of Columbia	State	State	General Assistance	Long-term	Disabled SSI applicants
Delaware	State	State	General Assistance	Long-term	Needy
Florida	County	County	General Assistance	Temporary	Disabled SSI applicants
Georgia	County	County	General Assistance	Temporary	Disabled SSI applicants
Kentucky	County	County	General Assistance	One-time	NA
Louisiana	State	State	General Assistance	Long-term	Disabled SSI applicants
Maryland	State, local	State, local	General Assistance	Long-term, temporary	Needy; Disabled SSI applicants
Mississippi	County	County	Emergency Assistance	NA	NA
North Carolina	County	County	Emergency Assistance	One-time	NA
Oklahoma	State	State	Emergency Assistance	One-time	NA
South Carolina	State	County	Emergency Assistance	Temporary	Disabled SSI applicants
Tennessee	County	County	Emergency Assistance	One-time	NA
Texas	County, local	County, local	General Assistance	One-time	NA
Virginia	Local, state	Local, state	General Assistance	Long-term	Disabled SSI applicants
West					
Alaska	State	State	Emergency Assistance	One-time	NA
Arizona	State	State	General Assistance	Long-term	Disabled SSI applicants
California	State, county	State, county	General Assistance	Long-term	Needy; Disabled SSI applicants
Colorado	State, county	State, county	Emergency Assistance	Long-term, one-time	NA Disabled SSI applicants

Table 7.1 (continued)

Region and state	Administrative control	Funding source	Program type	Duration of assistance available	Main recipients
West (continued)					
Hawaii	State	State	General Assistance	Long-term	Needy
Idaho	County	County	Emergency Assistance	One-time	NA
Montana	State, county	State	General Assistance	Long-term	Needy
Nevada	County	County	General Assistance	Temporary	Needy
New Mexico	State	State	General Assistance	Long-term	Needy
Oregon	State	State	General Assistance	Long-term	Disabled SSI applicants
Utah	State	State	General Assistance	Long-term	Needy
Washington	State	State	General Assistance	Long-term	Disabled SSI applicants
Wyoming	State	State	General Assistance	Temporary	Needy

Source: State and county documents; telephone interviews with state welfare officials.

NA = Not available.

Table 7.2 BASIC CHARACTERISTICS OF GENERAL ASSISTANCE PROGRAMS, BY STATE, FISCAL 1984

Region and state	Type of Payment		Whether standard of needs	Whether housing inspections
	Consolidated	Explicit		
Northeast				
Connecticut	X		Yes	Yes
Maine		X	Yes	No
Massachusetts	X		Yes	No
New Hampshire	X		(unclear)	No
New Jersey	X		Yes	No
New York		X	Yes	Yes
Pennsylvania	X		Yes	No
Rhode Island	X		Yes	Yes[a]
North Central				
Illinois	X		(unclear)	No
Iowa		X	Yes	No
Kansas		X	Yes	No
Michigan		X	Yes	No
Minnesota	X		Yes	No
Missouri	X		Yes	No
Nebraska	X[b]	X[c]	(unclear)	No
North Dakota		X[d]	(unclear)	No
Ohio		X	Yes	No
South Dakota		X	Yes	No
Wisconsin		X	(unclear)	Yes
South				
District of Columbia	X		Yes	No
Delaware	X		Yes	No
Florida	(unclear)		(unclear)	Yes
Georgia		X[e]	(unclear)	No
Kentucky		X	(unclear)	No
Louisiana	X		(unclear)	No
Maryland	X		Yes	No
Texas	X		(unclear)	No
Virginia	X		Yes	No
West				
Arizona		X	Yes	No
California		X	(unclear)	No
Hawaii		X	Yes	No
Montana	X		Yes	No
Nevada		X	(unclear)	No
New Mexico		X	Yes	No
Oregon		X	(unclear)	No
Utah		X	Yes	No
Washington	(unclear)		Yes	No
Wyoming	X		Yes	No

Source: State and county documents; telephone interviews with state welfare officials.

a. Mainly of rooming houses.
b. All of state except Omaha.
c. Omaha.
d. Burleigh County.
e. Fulton County.

Table 7.3 AGGREGATE INFORMATION ON GENERAL ASSISTANCE CASELOADS, RECIPIENTS, AND EXPENDITURES, FISCAL 1984

Region and state	Average caseload per month	Average recipients per month	Expenditures (dollars)		
			Total General Assistance	General Assistance shelter	Percent
Northeast					
Connecticut	22,602	29,441	58,173,425	37,060,290	64.0
Maine	5,212	10,949	8,189,797	6,273,465	77.0
Massachusetts	27,931	32,232	77,280,875	53,843,233	70.0
New Hampshire	1,036	1,244	1,689,845	844,923	50.0
New Jersey	30,427	31,014	46,367,880	26,893,370	58.0
New York	181,134	265,723	659,564,604	389,143,116	59.0
Pennsylvania	119,514	146,300	267,915,154	81,178,292	30.0
Rhode Island	4,457	6,149	11,500,107	6,670,062	58.0
Total Northeast	392,313	523,052	1,130,681,687	601,906,751	53.0
North Central					
Illinois	131,935	146,547	236,493,535	174,413,982	74.0
Iowa			1,953,904	1,465,428	75.0
Kansas	11,225	13,036	15,348,214	7,531,994	49.0
Michigan	148,720	177,584	350,040,000	245,670,275	70.0
Minnesota	14,938	16,537	43,615,388	29,658,464	68.0
Missouri	5,036	5,136	5,408,826	4,327,061	80.0
Nebraska	726	1,065	1,373,012	964,962	70.0
North Dakota	141	290	277,088	204,379	90.0
Ohio	151,003	164,976	192,293,754	96,146,877	50.0
South Dakota			272,776	109,630	40.0
Wisconsin	22,418	25,047	38,167,411	19,465,380	51.0
Total North Central	486,142	550,218	885,193,908	579,958,432	66.0

Table 7.3 (continued)

Region and state	Average caseload per month	Average recipients per month	Expenditures (dollars)		
			Total General Assistance	General Assistance shelter	Percent
South					
District of Columbia	5,483	5,671	13,076,000	6,668,760	51.0
Delaware	2,295	3,633	3,432,539	2,071,360	60.0
Florida			3,600,000	2,700,000	75.0
Georgia	2,598	3,750	1,853,831	1,186,451	64.0
Kentucky	380	557	889,280	642,000	72.0
Louisiana	3,367	3,367	3,740,850	2,169,693	58.0
Maryland	21,208	22,161	32,478,499	17,051,212	53.0
Texas	3,408	5,000	4,540,000	2,769,400	61.0
Virginia	7,501	10,205	10,785,848	5,716,499	53.0
Total South	46,240	54,344	74,396,847	40,975,847	55.0
West					
Arizona	4,274	4,313	6,243,720	1,729,030	28.0
California	62,204	71,070	138,964,579	87,547,685	63.0
Hawaii	5,724	8,424	18,376,205	10,841,961	59.0
Montana	1,399	1,399	2,322,493	1,416,721	61.0
Nevada	278	408	496,788	140,756	28.0
New Mexico	445	653	1,084,830	658,380	61.0
Oregon	3,755	5,509	5,376,501	3,716,799	69.0
Utah	2,213	3,795	5,712,862	3,238,166	57.0
Washington	13,463	13,569	32,143,500	20,038,828	62.0
Wyoming	625	917	1,891,474	775,504	41.0
Total West	94,398	110,056	212,612,952	130,103,829	61.0

Table 7.3 (continued)

Region	Average caseload per month	Average recipients per month	Expenditures (dollars) Total General Assistance	General Assistance shelter	Percent
Northeast	392,313	523,052	1,130,681,687	601,906,751	53.0
North Central	486,142	550,218	885,193,908	579,958,432	66.0
South	46,240	54,344	74,396,847	40,975,375	55.0
West	94,398	110,056	212,612,952	130,103,829	61.0
National total	1,019,093	1,237,670	2,302,885,394	1,352,944,387	59.0

Source: State and county documents; telephone interviews with state officials.

1. The following states were deleted from the tabulations because they did not have a General Assistance program in fiscal 1984: Alaska, Arkansas, Colorado, Idaho, Mississippi, North Carolina, Oklahoma, Tennessee, Vermont, and West Virginia. It should be noted, however, that the majority of these states did offer some form of short-term Emergency Assistance.

2. Incomplete or no response was received from Alabama, Indiana, and South Carolina. These states, therefore, do not appear in the tabulations.

3. The following assumptions were used to assign data to missing cells, by state. New Hampshire: 1983, number of cases; 1984, number of recipients. New Jersey: Aggregate and actual shelter percents and dollars based on the national averages of aggregate and actual shelter percents for all states with complete data on each of these items, weighted by number of recipients per state. New York: Number of cases based on national ratio of recipients to cases among those states with complete data on each of these items. Rhode Island: Aggregate and actual shelter percents and dollars based on national averages for all states with complete data on each of these items, weighted by number of recipients per state. Iowa: (a) Aggregate GA dollars based on assumption that Polk County expenditures equal 27 percent of state expenditures. These expenditures were then blown up to state aggregates. (b) Polk County aggregate shelter percent was used as estimate of the state's shelter percent. (c) Actual shelter dollars and percent represent Polk County. Missouri: (a) Aggregate shelter percent and dollars derived from telephone interviews. (b) Actual shelter percent assumed to equal aggregate shelter percent. Number of recipients based on state official's view that only about 100 cases included two persons. Nebraska: (a) Aggregate GA dollars based on assumption that Omaha represents 50 percent of state expenditures on GA. These expenditures were blown up to state aggregates. (b) Number of recipients based on national ratio of cases to recipients among those states with complete data on each of these items. North Dakota: Aggregate shelter percent derived from telephone interviews (no state documentation available). Actual GA and shelter payments represent Burleigh County. South Dakota: Aggregate shelter percent assigned to actual shelter percent.

Table 7.3 (continued)

Wisconsin: (a) Actual GA and shelter dollars represent Milwaukee. (b) Milwaukee County aggregate shelter percent used to estimate state's shelter percent. Florida: Aggregate GA and shelter dollars based on telephone interviews. Actual GA and shelter dollars represent Miami. Georgia: Aggregate GA dollars, number of cases, and number of recipients assumes Fulton County represents 80 percent of each of these quantities for the state. These numbers were then blown up to state estimates. Kentucky: Number of recipients based on national ratio of cases to recipients among those states with complete data on each of these items. Louisiana: (a) Aggregate and actual shelter percents based on the national averages for all states with complete data on each of these items, weighted by number of recipients per state. (b) All other entries in table based on telephone interviews (no state documentation available). Maryland: (a) Aggregate and actual shelter dollars derived from telephone interviews. (b) Estimates represent the combination of two GA programs in the state: one for "unemployables" and the other for "employables." Texas: (a) Aggregate dollars represent the combination of expenditures by several Texas counties. (b) Aggregate percent of GA to shelter assumed to equal actual shelter percent. (c) Number of recipients derived from telephone interviews. (d) Number of cases based on national ratio of recipients to cases among those states with complete data on each of these items. (e) Actual GA and shelter dollars based on Harris County (Houston). Montana: (a) Aggregate shelter percent assumed to equal actual shelter percent. (b) State documents show average number of cases equals average number of recipients. (c) Actual shelter dollars represent an average for counties in the state, as reported in telephone interviews. Nevada: (a) Aggregate GA dollars represent a combination of Clark and Washoe Counties which reportedly account for roughly 90 percent of state GA dollars. (b) Number of recipients based on assumption that Washoe recipients represent 20 percent of the state's GA recipients. This number was then blown up to an estimate of the total number of recipients in the state. (c) Number of cases based on national ratio of recipients to cases among those states with complete data on each of these items. (d) Actual GA and shelter dollars represent Clark County. New Mexico: Number of cases based on national ratio of recipients to cases among those states with complete data on each of these items. Oregon: Number of recipients based on national ratio of cases to recipients among those states with complete data on each of these items. Wyoming: Number of cases based on national ratio of recipients to cases among those states with complete data on each of these items.

4. Data assignments were not made in cases where states were missing pairs of variables such as cases and recipients, or actual total and shelter GA payments.

5. Regional and national GA-shelter dollars include some states where this value was assigned based on various assumptions. See listing under note 3 for details.

6. Regional and national percents of GA dollars for shelter (both aggregate and actual payments) are weighted by the number of recipients in each state.

7. Regional estimates of actual GA and GA-shelter payments are weighted by the number of recipients in each state.

8. Shelter amounts include rent and utilities.

Table 7.4   SUMMARY STATISTICS ON SHELTER ASSISTANCE UNDER GENERAL ASSISTANCE, BY STATE, FISCAL 1984 (dollars unless otherwise indicated)

Region and state	Payment per person			HUD Fair Market Rent (0 bedroom, min.)	General Assistance / Fair Market Rent (percent)
	Total General Assistance	General Assistance shelter	Percent		
Northeast					
Connecticut	268	176	66.0	239	74.0
Maine	406	311	77.0	248	125.0
Massachusetts	244	169	69.0	261	65.0
New Jersey	200	120	60.0	265	45.0
New York	287	193	67.0	191	101.0
Pennsylvania	177	54	30.0	155	35.0
Rhode Island	276	166	60.0	267	62.0
Total weighted average	250	149	60.0	194	77.0
North Central					
Illinois	154	114	74.0	169	67.0
Iowa	280	210	75.0	201	104.0
Kansas	216	106	49.0	159	67.0
Michigan	218	153	70.0	208	74.0
Minnesota	236	173	73.0	195	89.0
Missouri	80	64	80.0	159	40.0
Nebraska	240	225	94.0	188	120.0
North Dakota	210	200	95.0	207	97.0
Ohio	128	64	50.0	155	41.0
South Dakota	125	50	40.0	199	25.0
Wisconsin	175	78	45.0	188	41.0
Total weighted average	171	111	65.0	179	62.0

Table 7.4 (continued)

| Region and state | Payment per person | | | HUD Fair Market Rent (0 bedroom, min.) | General Assistance / Fair Market Rent (percent) |
	Total General Assistance	General Assistance shelter	Percent		
South					
Delaware	116	70	60.0	244	29.0
District of Columbia	210	107	51.0	319	34.0
Florida	180	108	60.0	198	55.0
Georgia	225	145	64.0	184	79.0
Kentucky	140	100	71.0	169	59.0
Louisiana	91	55	60.0	156	35.0
Maryland	126	59	47.0	244	24.0
Texas	109	66	61.0	167	40.0
Virginia	157	83	53.0	183	45.0
Total weighted average	144	77	53.0	222	35.0
West					
Arizona	130	36	28.0	233	15.0
California	228	143	63.0	237	60.0
Hawaii	297	175	59.0	370	47.0
Montana	212	130	61.0	225	58.0
Nevada	228	57	25.0	297	19.0
New Mexico	145	88	61.0	197	45.0
Oregon	212	147	69.0	200	74.0
Utah	217	123	57.0	192	64.0
Washington	303	189	62.0	236	80.0
Wyoming	145	60	41.0	214	28.0
Total weighted average	236	145	61.0	243	60.0

Table 7.4 (continued)

| Region and state | Payment per person | | | HUD Fair Market Rent (0 bedroom, min.) | General Assistance / Fair Market Rent (percent) |
	Total General Assistance	General Assistance shelter	Percent		
Northeast	250	149	60.0	194	77.0
North Central	171	111	65.0	179	62.0
South	144	77	53.0	222	35.0
West	236	145	61.0	243	60.0
National total weighted average	209	129	62.0	193	67.0

Source: State and county documents; telephone interviews with state officials.

1. The following states were deleted from the tabulations because they did not have a General Assistance program in fiscal 1984: Alaska, Arkansas, Colorado, Idaho, Mississippi, North Carolina, Oklahoma, Tennessee, Vermont, and West Virginia. It should be noted, however, that the majority of these states did offer some form of short-term Emergency Assistance.

2. Incomplete or no response was received from Alabama, Indiana, and South Carolina. These states, therefore, do not appear in the tabulations.

3. Persons assumed to equal recipients.

4. The following assumptions were used to assign data to missing cells, by state. New Jersey: Actual shelter percents and dollars based on the national averages of actual shelter percents for all states with complete data on each of these items, weighted by number of recipients per state. New York: Number of cases based on national ratio of recipients to cases among those states with complete data on each of these items. Rhode Island: Actual shelter percents and dollars based on national averages for all states with complete data on each of these items, weighted by number of recipients per state. Iowa: Actual shelter dollars and percent represent Polk County. Missouri: (a) Actual shelter percent assumed to equal aggregate shelter percent. (b) Number of recipients based on state official's view that only about 100 cases included two persons. Nebraska: Number of recipients based on national ratio of cases to recipients among those states with complete data on each of these items. North Dakota: Actual GA and shelter payments represent Burleigh County. South Dakota: Aggregate shelter percent assigned to actual shelter percent. Wisconsin: Actual GA and shelter dollars represent Milwaukee.

Table 7.4 (continued)

Florida: Actual GA and shelter dollars represent Miami. Georgia: Based on Fulton County. Kentucky: Number of recipients based on national ratio of cases to recipients among those states with complete data on each of these items. Louisiana: (a) Actual shelter percents based on the national averages for all states with complete data on each of these items, weighted by number of recipients per state. (b) All other entries in table based on telephone interviews (no state documentation available). Maryland: (a) Actual shelter dollars derived from telephone interviews. (b) Estimates represent the combination of two GA programs in the state: one for "unemployables" and the other for "employables." Texas: (a) Number of recipients derived from telephone interviews. (b) Actual GA and shelter dollars based on Harris County (Houston). Montana: (a) State documents show average number of cases equals average number of recipients. (b) Actual shelter dollars represent an average for counties in the state, as reported in telephone interviews. Nevada: (a) Number of recipients based on assumption that Washoe recipients represent 20 percent of the state's GA recipients. This number was then blown up to an estimate of the total number of recipients in the state. (b) Actual GA and shelter dollars represent Clark County. Oregon: Number of recipients based on national ratio of cases to recipients among those states with complete data on each of these items.

4. Data assignments were not made in cases where states were missing pairs of variables such as cases and recipients, or actual total and shelter GA payments.

5. Regional and national GA-shelter dollars include some states where this value was assigned based on various assumptions. See listing under note 3 for details.

6. Regional and national percents of GA actual dollars for shelter are weighted by the number of recipients in each state.

7. Regional estimates of actual GA and GA-shelter payments are weighted by the number of recipients in each state.

8. Shelter amounts include rent and utilities.

Table 7.5 GENERAL ASSISTANCE TOTAL AND SHELTER PAYMENTS BY FAMILY SIZE, FISCAL 1984

Region and state	Shelter (percent)	Total payment (dollars)				Shelter payment (dollars)			
		Family size				Family size			
		One	Two	Three	Four	One	Two	Three	Four
Northeast									
Connecticut	66.0	268	NA	NA	NA	176	NA	NA	NA
Maine	77.0	406	471	593	649	311	311	365	365
Massachusetts	69.0	244	318	391	465	169	170	170	170
New Jersey	43.0	200	275	275	275	86	118	118	118
New York	67.0	287	377	444	528	193	227	244	270
Pennsylvania	30.0	177	273	348	429	54	83	105	130
Rhode Island	60.0	276	376	464	528	166	266	278	317
Total weighted average	56.0	250	338	405	481	147	176	193	215
North Central									
Illinois	74.0	154	NA	NA	NA	114	NA	NA	NA
Iowa	75.0	280	359	397	448	210	268	298	336
Kansas	49.0	216	280	338	385	106	106	106	106
Michigan	70.0	218	242	309	349	153	170	216	244
Minnesota	73.0	236	305	353	395	173	201	218	226
Missouri	80.0	80	80	80	80	64	NA	NA	NA
Nebraska	94.0	240	280	350	420	225	250	290	330
North Dakota	95.0	210	260	320	370	200	250	300	350
Ohio	50.0	128	168	196	244	64	88	93	106
South Dakota	40.0	125	140	175	175	50	56	70	70
Wisconsin	45.0	175	NA	NA	NA	78	NA	NA	NA
Total weighted average	44.0	130	212	260	303	81	131	156	175

Table 7.5 (continued)

Region and state	Shelter (percent)	Total payment (dollars)				Shelter payment (dollars)			
		Family size				Family size			
		One	Two	Three	Four	One	Two	Three	Four
South									
District of Columbia	51.0	210	257	257	257	107	131	131	131
Delaware	60.0	116	161	217	255	70	97	130	153
Florida	60.0	180	NA	NA	NA	108	NA	NA	NA
Georgia	64.0	225	337	181	174	145	197	101	94
Kentucky	71.0	140	160	200	230	100	100	112	126
Louisiana	60.0	91	91	91	91	55	55	55	55
Maryland	47.0	126	171	218	NA	59	80	103	NA
Texas	61.0	109	109	201	201	66	66	122	122
Virginia	53.0	157	231	291	347	83	83	84	83
Total weighted average	53.0	143	191	224	249	76	76	114	124
West									
Arizona	28.0	130	180	233	282	36	39	50	62
California	63.0	228	228	228	514	143	143	143	234
Hawaii	59.0	297	390	468	546	175	215	240	265
Montana	61.0	212	284	358	432	130	173	218	264
Nevada	25.0	228	308	388	468	57	77	97	117
New Mexico	61.0	145	145	210	210	88	88	88	88
Oregon	69.0	212	280	280	280	147	162	162	162
Utah	57.0	217	301	376	439	123	154	178	190
Washington	62.0	303	383	474	558	189	218	255	285
Wyoming	41.0	145	235	260	285	60	85	65	60
Total weighted average	61.0	236	263	287	494	145	154	163	229

Table 7.5 (continued)

Region	Shelter (percent)	Total payment (dollars) Family size				Shelter payment (dollars) Family size			
		One	Two	Three	Four	One	Two	Three	Four
Northeast	56.0	250	338	405	481	147	176	193	215
North Central	44.0	130	212	260	303	81	131	156	175
South	53.0	143	191	224	249	76	102	114	124
West	61.0	236	263	287	494	145	154	163	228
National total weighted average	51.0	191	276	330	409	114	154	172	199

Source: State and county documents; telephone interviews with state officials.

NA = Not available. This designation is used in states where no information could be retrieved on whether total General Assistance payment varied by family size and, if so, by how much.

1. The following states were deleted from the tabulations because they did not have a General Assistance program in fiscal 1984: Alaska, Arkansas, Colorado, Idaho, Mississippi, North Carolina, Oklahoma, Tennessee, Vermont, and West Virginia. It should be noted, however, that the majority of these states did offer some form of short-term Emergency Assistance.
2. Information on actual General Assistance total and shelter dollars was not obtained from Alabama, Indiana, New Hampshire, and South Carolina.
3. Percents shown represent shelter: total General Assistance for one-person unit.

Table 7.5 (continued)

4. The assumptions used to complete the tabulations for states with missing or problematic data are as follows. New Jersey: (a) Amounts shown are for the GA program for unemployable persons. (b) Total GA for three and four person households in three and four person eligible units based on percent increases in need standard for the GA program for employables. (Comparable data were not available for the GA-unemployables program.) (c) Actual shelter payment percent based on national average. Rhode Island: Actual shelter payment percent based on national average. Iowa: (a) Information shown represents Polk County. (b) We assumed that the 75 percent shelter: total GA applied across all family sizes. Michigan: We assumed that the 70 percent shelter: total GA applied across all family sizes. South Dakota: (a) Actual shelter percent represents the aggregate percent of GA dollars that the state spends on shelter. (b) We assumed that the 40 percent shelter: total GA applied across all family sizes. Georgia: The two person family shown represents the state's payment to "couples." The three and four person amounts shown represent payments for an individual "who is living with three or four others." Louisiana: (a) Actual GA shelter percent based on the national average for all states with complete data on this item, weighted by the number of recipients per state. We assumed the 60 percent shelter: total GA applied across all family sizes. Missouri: Actual shelter percent assumed to equal aggregate shelter percent. Nevada: Data shown represents Clark County.

Regional averages are weighted by the number of recipients in each state.

CITATIONS

1. New York Times. Editorial, "A Street is Not a Home." 24 August 1984.

2. New York Times. "Failure of Plan for Homeless Reflects City Housing Crisis." 19 February 1985.

3. Johnson, Sara, and National Low Income Housing Coalition. 1986. Summary of Low Income Housing Tax Credit Provisions, presented at "New Frontiers in Housing Tax Conference." Washington, D.C.: National Low Income Housing Coalition.

4. Nenno, Mary. "What is the Future for Federal Housing Assistance?" Washington, D.C.: NAHRO (May 1983), processed.

5. U.S. House of Representatives, Committee on Ways and Means. February 1985. Background Material and Data on Programs Within the Jurisdiction of the Committee on Ways and Means. Washington, D.C.

6. Social Security Administration. 1985. The SSI Program for the Aged, Blind, and Disabled: Characteristics of State Assistance Programs for SSI Recipients, January 1985. Baltimore.

7. Duncan, Greg. personal communication (October 1986).

8. National Housing Law Project. 1985. HUD Housing Programs. Berkeley, Calif.

9. Newman, S., and M. Owen. 1982. Residential Displacement in the U.S.: 1970-1977. Ann Arbor, Mich.: University of Michigan, Institute for Social Research.

10. Bradbury, K., and A. Downs, editors. 1986. Do Housing Allowances Work? Washington, D.C.: Brookings.

11. Lowry, I., editor. 1983. Experimenting with Housing Allowances. Cambridge, Mass.: Oelgeschlager, Gunn, and Hain.

URBAN INSTITUTE REPORT Series

Urban Institute Reports are used to disseminate quickly significant research findings and analyses arising out of the work of The Urban Institute. To reduce costs and minimize production delays, these reports are produced with desktop publishing technology after rigorous review according to the highest standards of policy research and analysis.

1. **Subsidizing Shelter: The Relationship Between Welfare and Housing Assistance**
   Part 1: **Analysis and Findings**
   Part 2: **Data Book**

2. **Future U.S. Housing Policy**
   Raymond J. Struyk, Makiko Ueno, and Margery Turner

3. **Income Security in America: The Record and the Prospects**
   John L. Palmer

4. **Assessing Housing Needs and Policy Alternatives in Developing Countries**
   Raymond J. Struyk

- -

Please send me information on the new **URBAN INSTITUTE REPORT** Series.

_____
Name

_____
Street address

_____
City   State   Zip code

Return to: Sheila Dell
      The Urban Institute
      Order Department
      4720 Boston Way, Lanham, Md. 20706

- -